# Sannel Larson's Busy, Bumbazing Bees

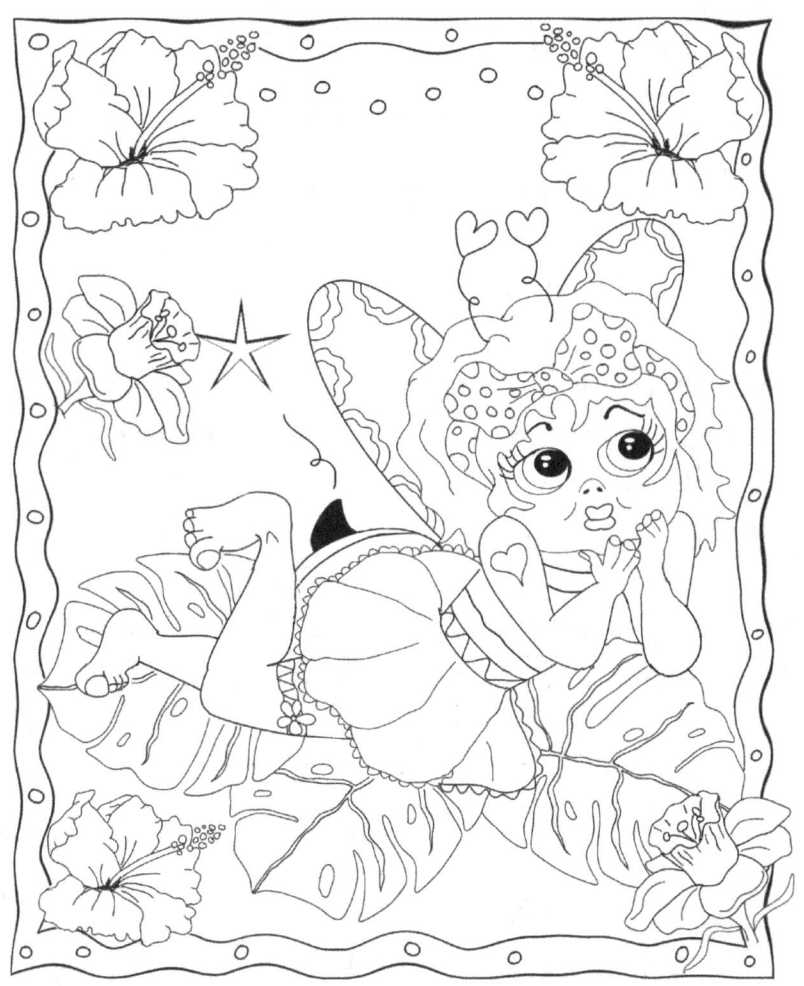

## Coloring Book

# Sannel Larson's
# Busy, Bumbazing Bees
## Coloring Book

Copyright © 2017 Sannel Larson
Illustrations copyright ©2017 Sannel Larson
All rights reserved.

No part of this book may be stored in a retrieval system, reproduced or transmitted by any form or by any means, electronic, mechanical, photocopying, recording, or otherwise without a written permission from the copyright holder, in this case the author and artist of the publication, except while giving brief quotations in the articles and reviews.

ISBN-13: 978-1975914745

ISBN-10: 1975914740

Illustrated by artist
Sannel Larson

# In order of apperances

Page:

1 Bumblissa
3 Bumbusing
5 Blossomling
7 Queen Rumblizabeth
9 Waddlebee
11 Tumbazing
13 Bumblestumble
15 Wingbuzzing
17 Bumby
19 Bumblightful
21 Mumbusing
23 Yummy Le Bee
25 Mumblightful
27 Queen Bumbleroyal
29 Delbumble
31 Bumbladorable

33 Stingling
35 Bumblossom
37 Queen Royalbee
39 Bumbluptuous
41 Blossomling
43 Bumblacious
45 Stumblebee
47 Mumb Le Bee
49 Blossom Le Bee
51 Awesome Le Bee
53 Lovablebee
55 Bumbosia
57 Beedorable
59 Pollen Le Bee

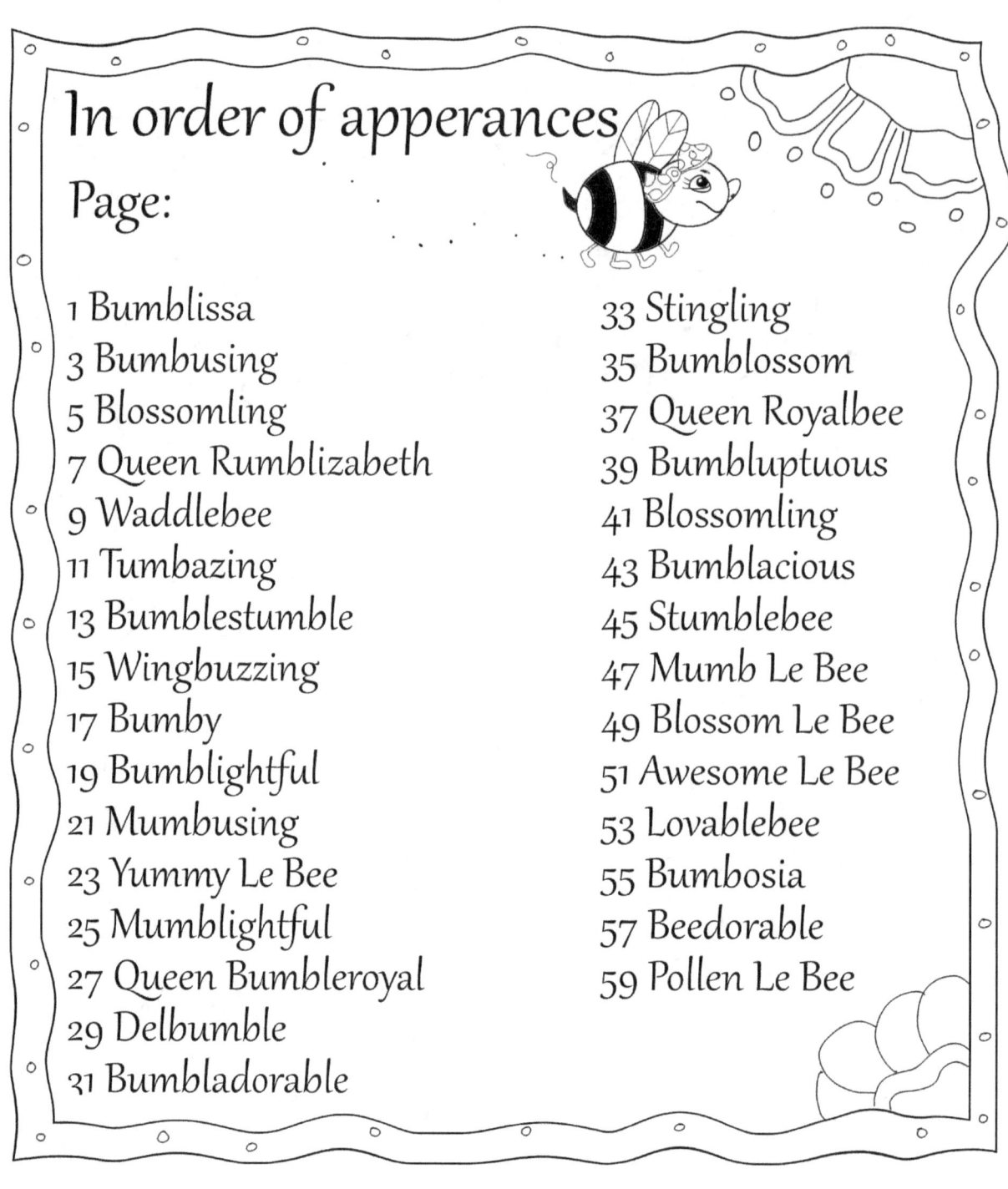

A Note From The Artist...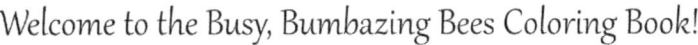

Welcome to the Busy, Bumbazing Bees Coloring Book!

Thank you to everyone for purchasing my fantasy fun coloring book. All these bumbladorable, hand-drawn illustrations for this coloring book were created with much fun, care and love. I hope you enjoy coloring it as much as I enjoyed creating it.

Please, don't forget to leave a review of this book, as well as to share your bee-autiful, bumbazing, colorful bee art on amazon.com. I would love to see Queen Royalbee, Queen Rumblizabeth, Queen Bumbleroyal and their buzzing working girls in color.

All the illustrations are single-sided so you don't have to worry about ruining a design on the opposite page. However, I would suggest placing a piece of paper or two under the page you are coloring, and the illustration beneath will be fully protected. So go ahead and use markers, colored pencils, fine point markers, crayons and pastels.

Use the finished pages to send to friends and family in place of "Thinking of You" cards, "Get Well" cards, or cards just to make them smile.

Happy art making everyone!

Sannel

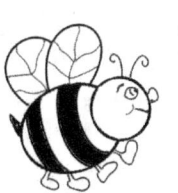
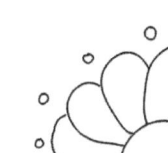

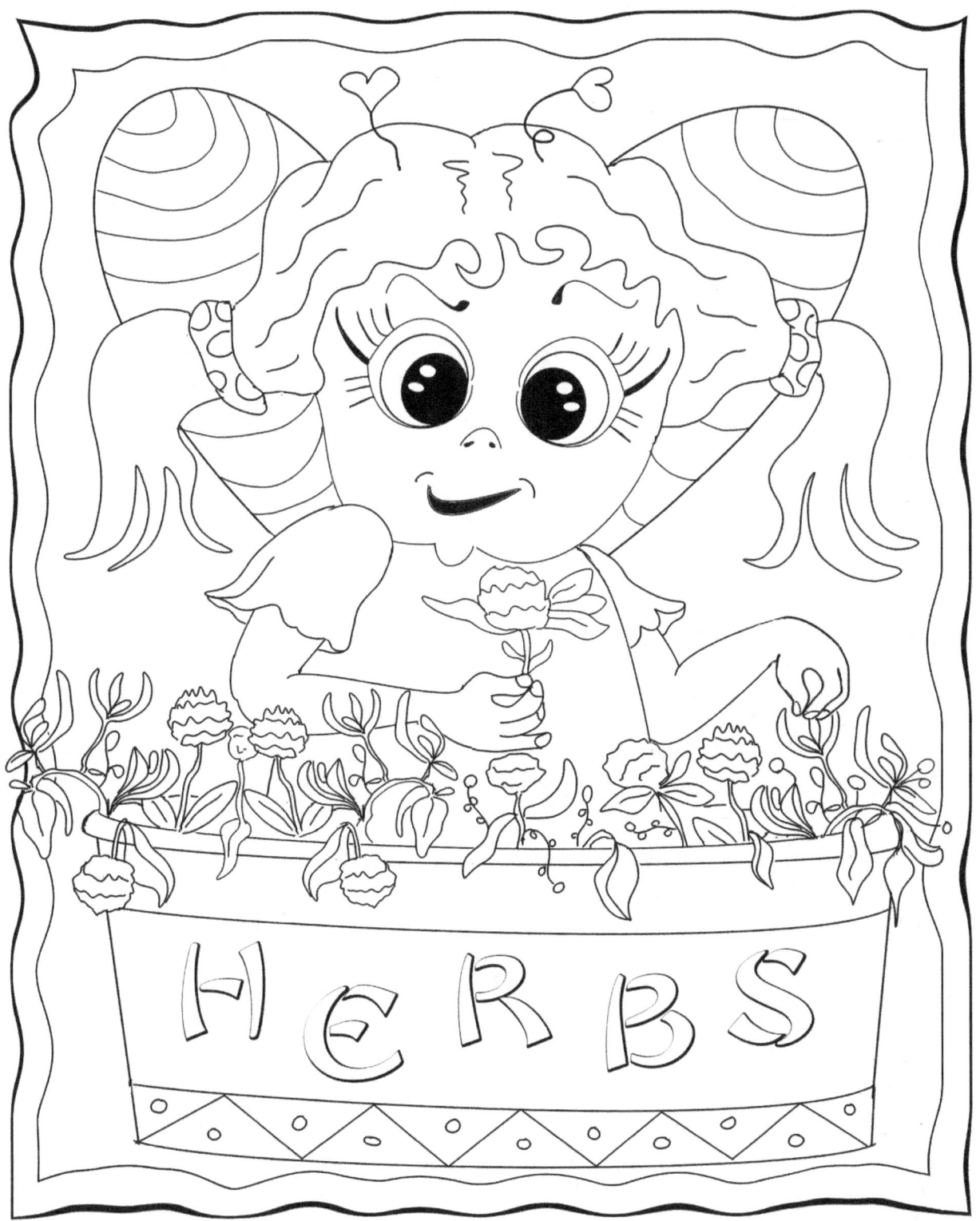

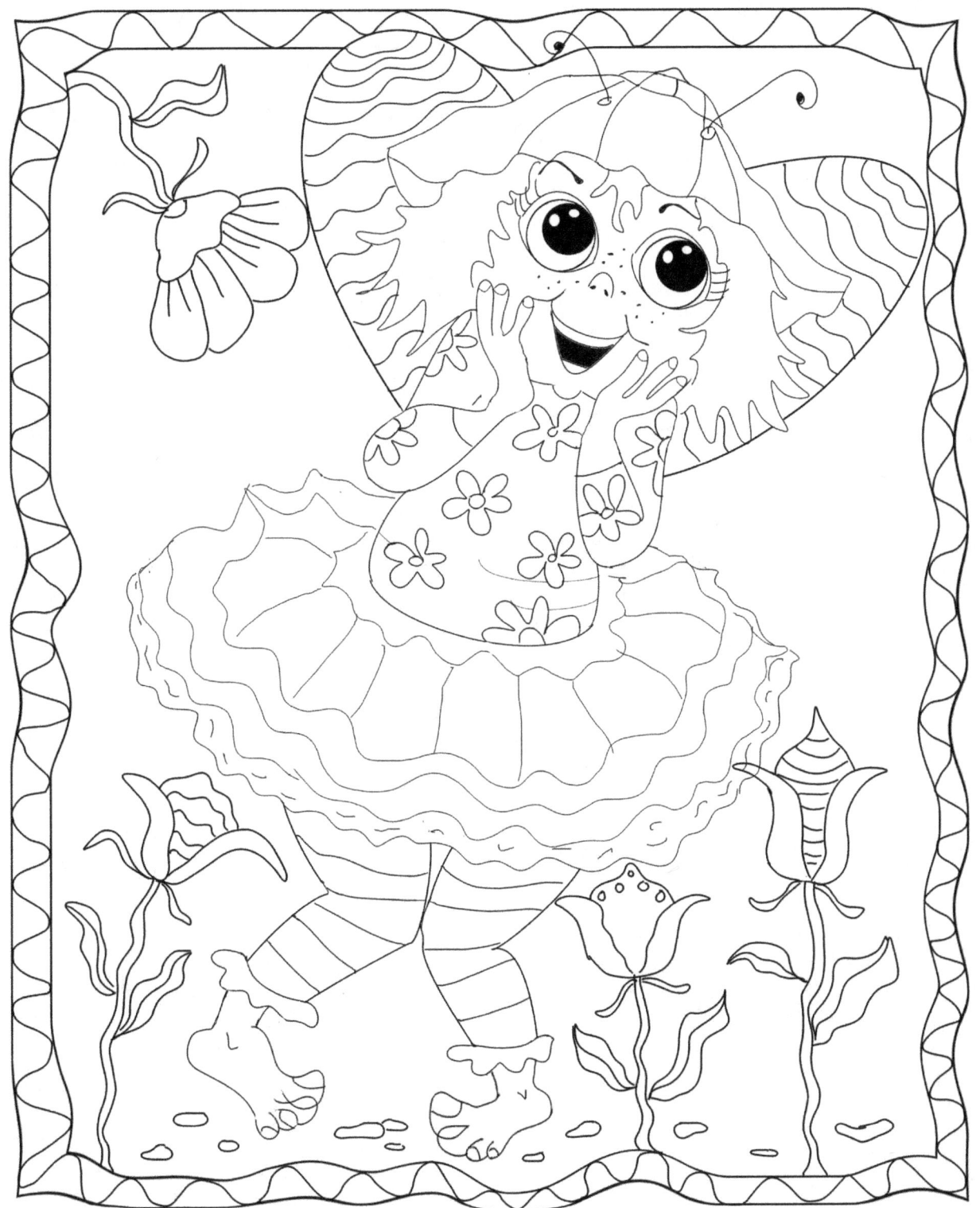

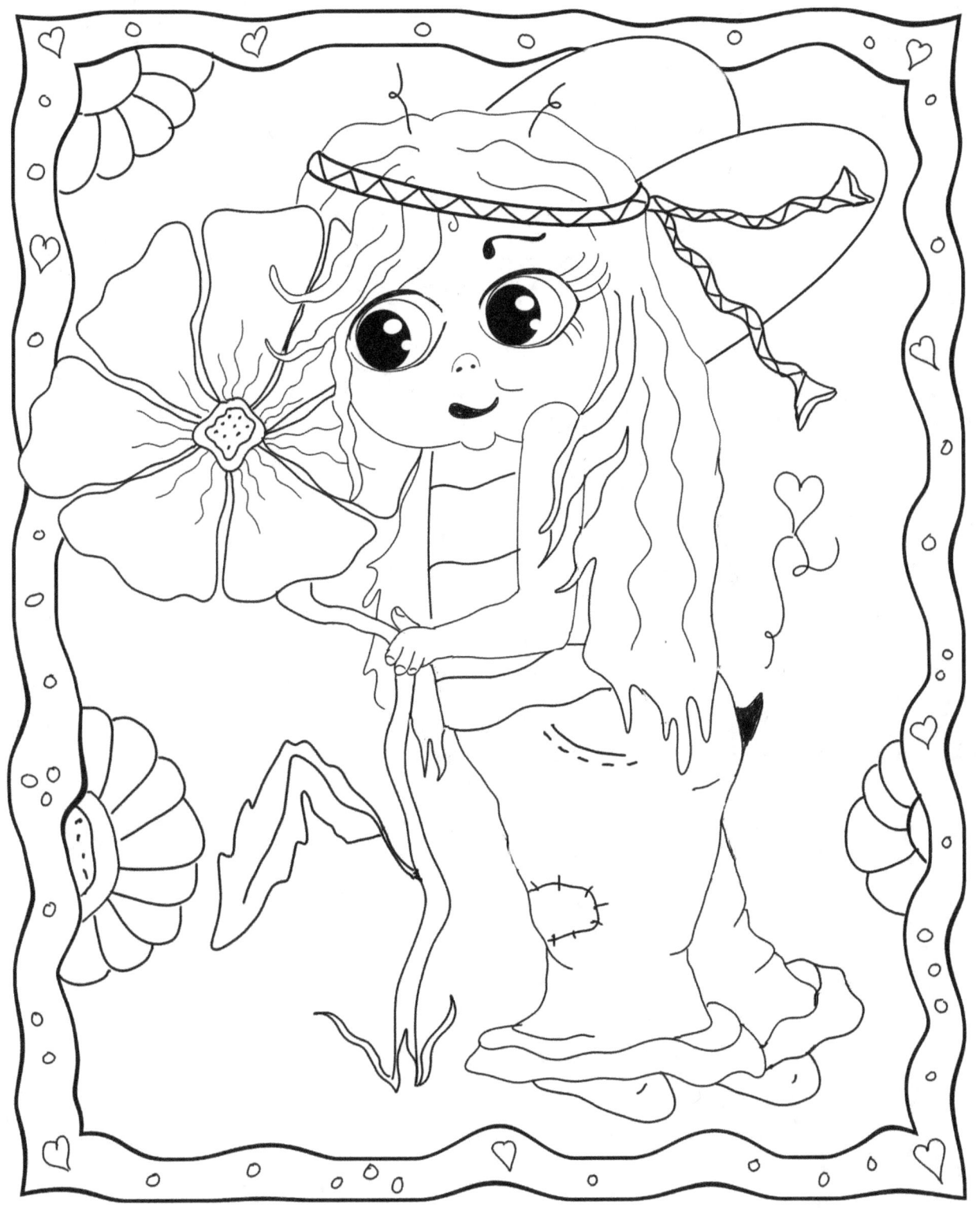

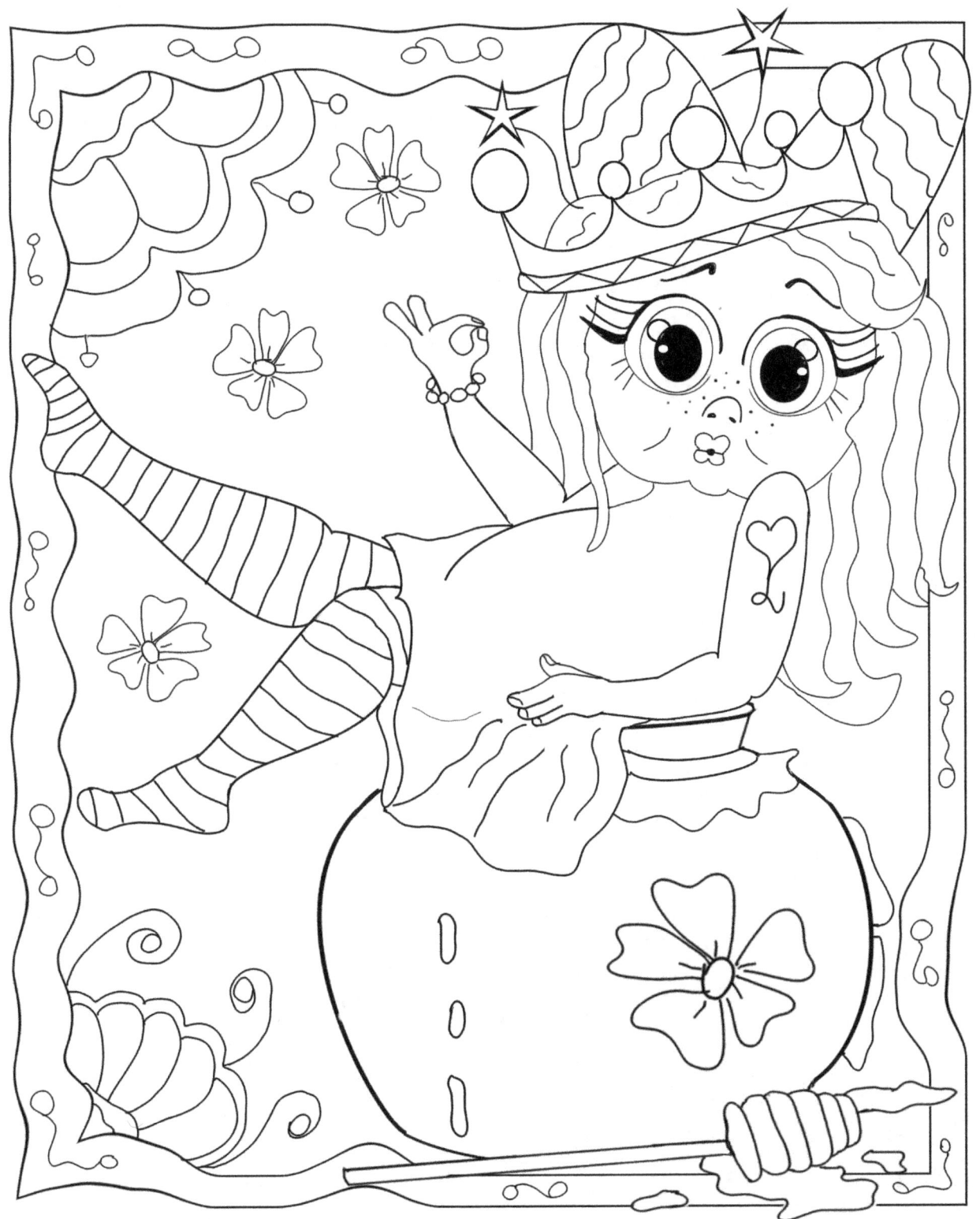

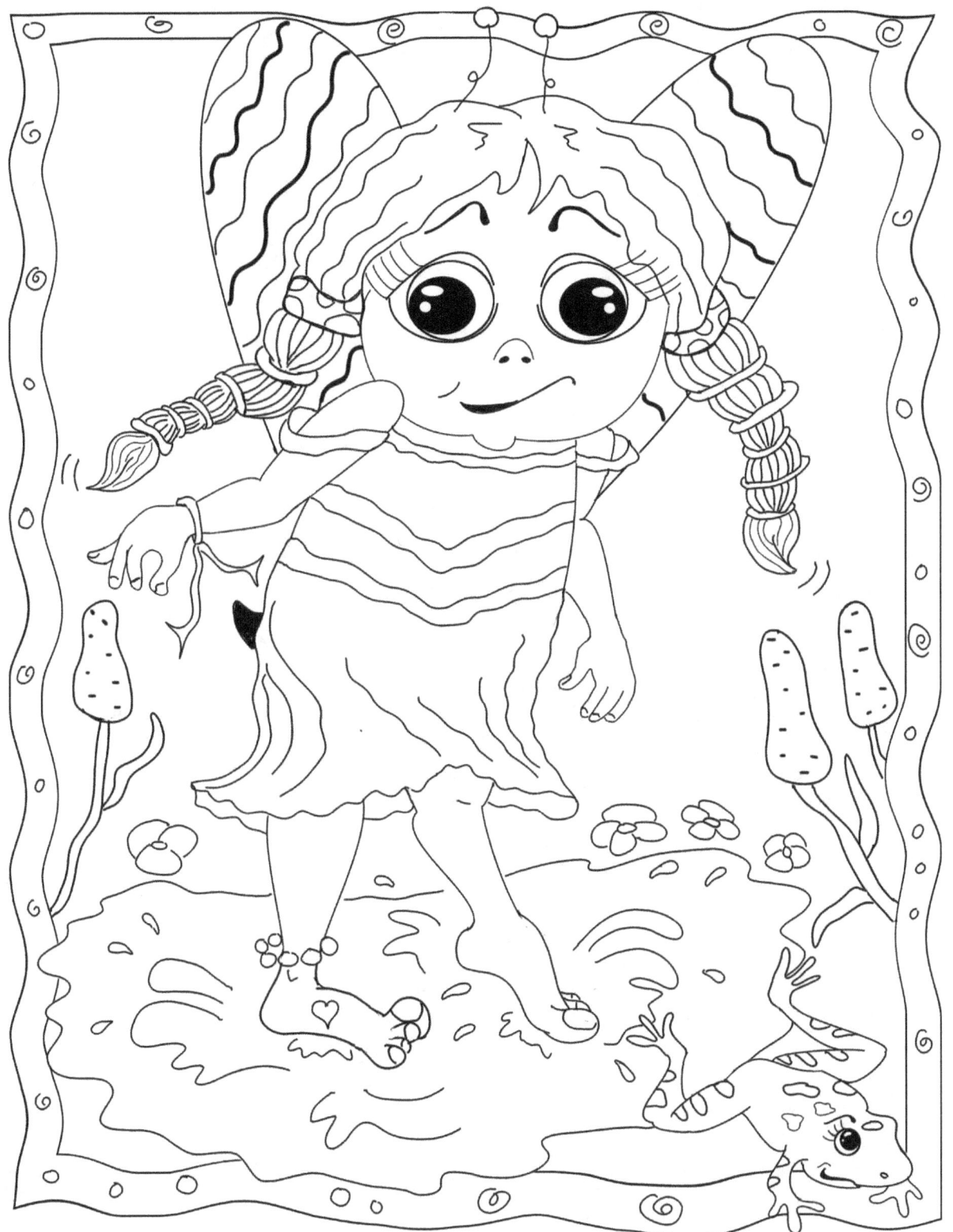

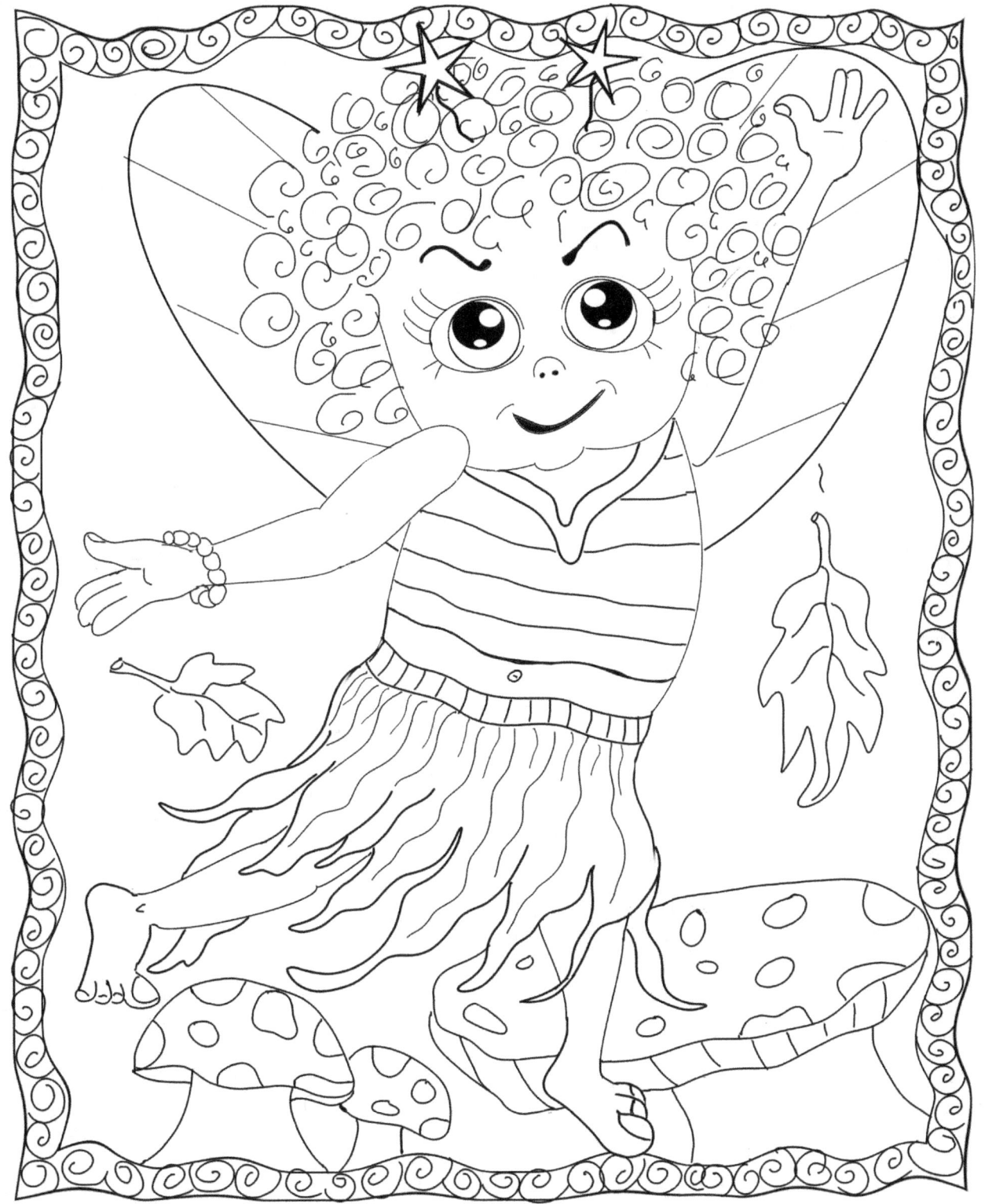

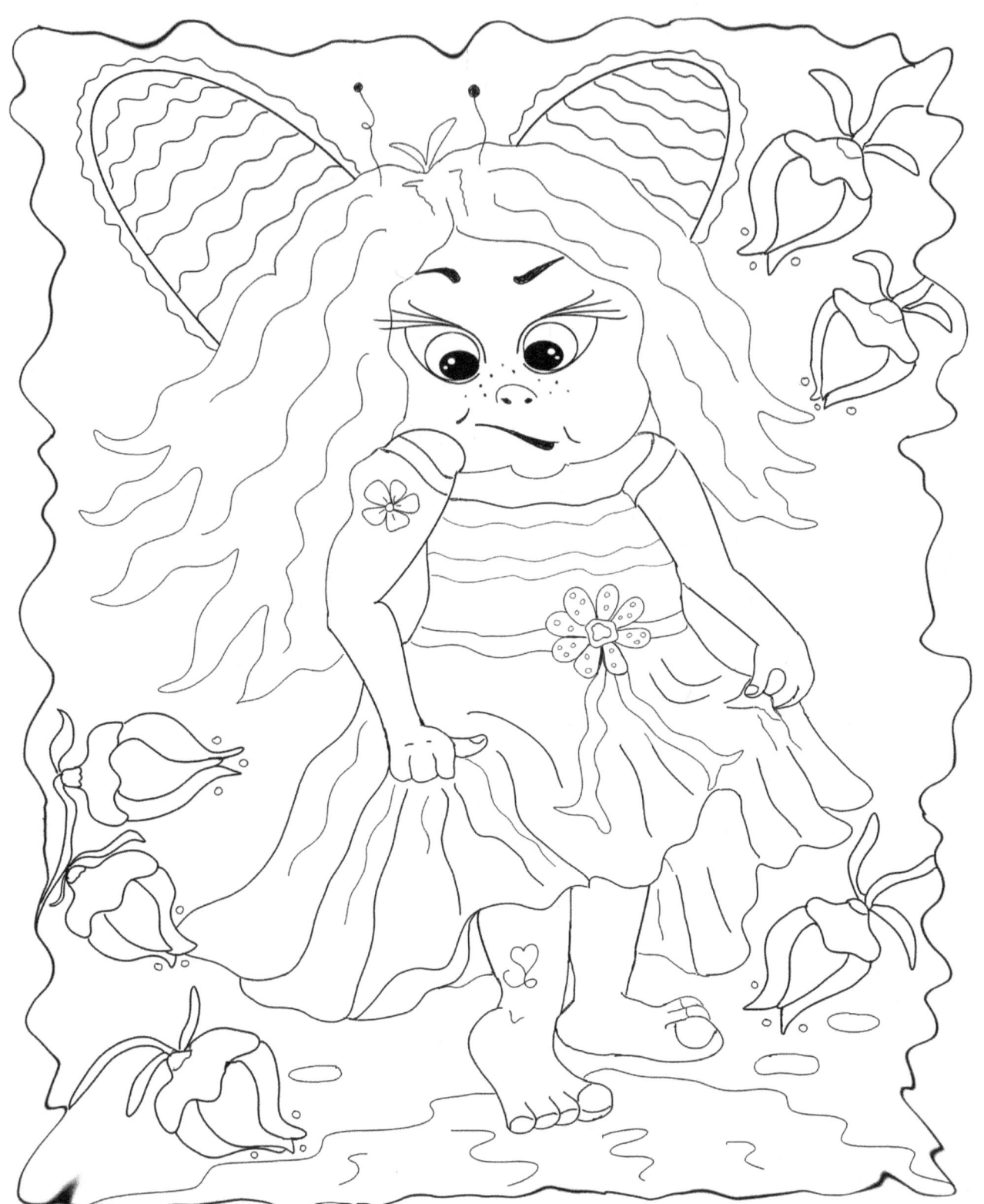

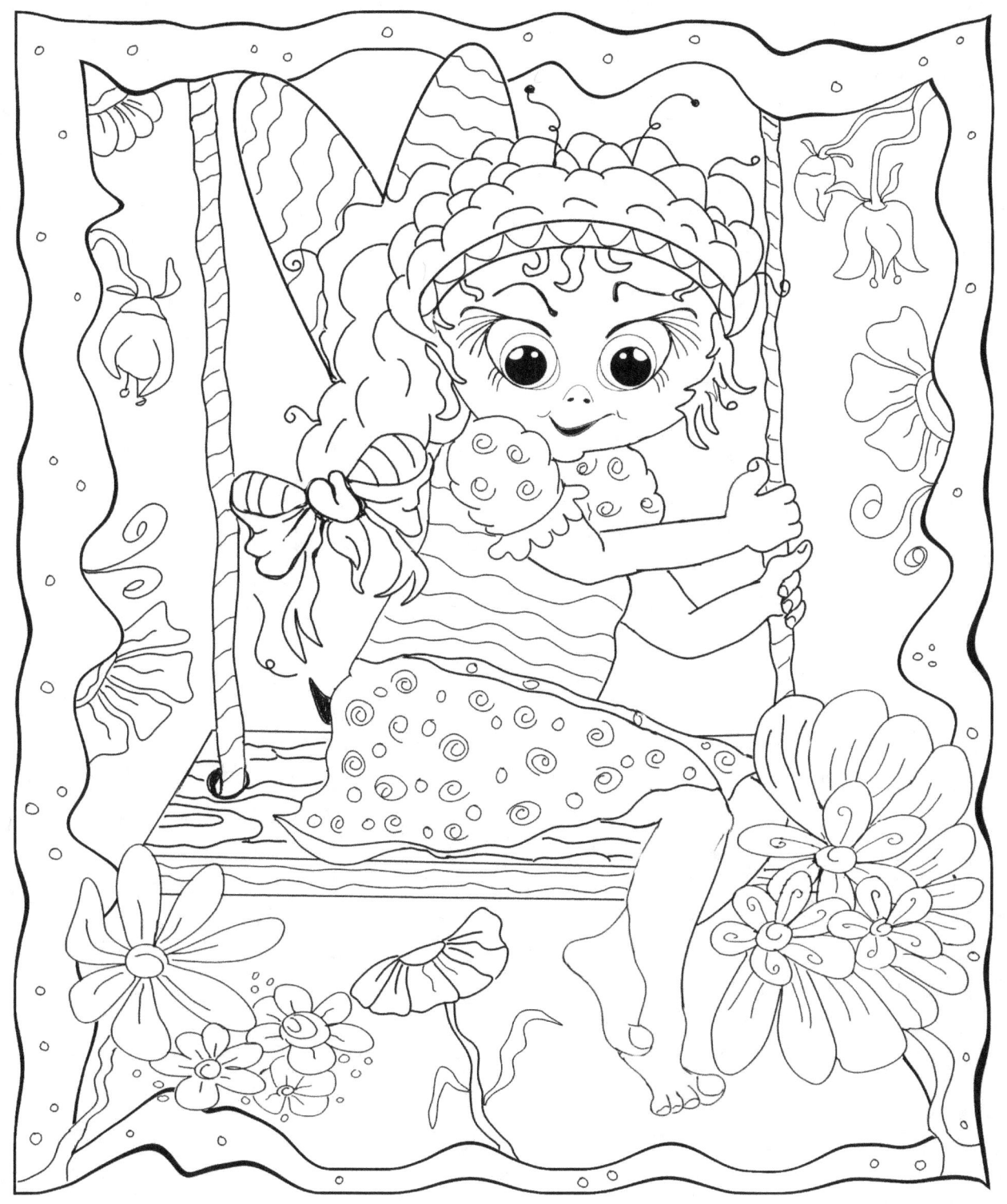

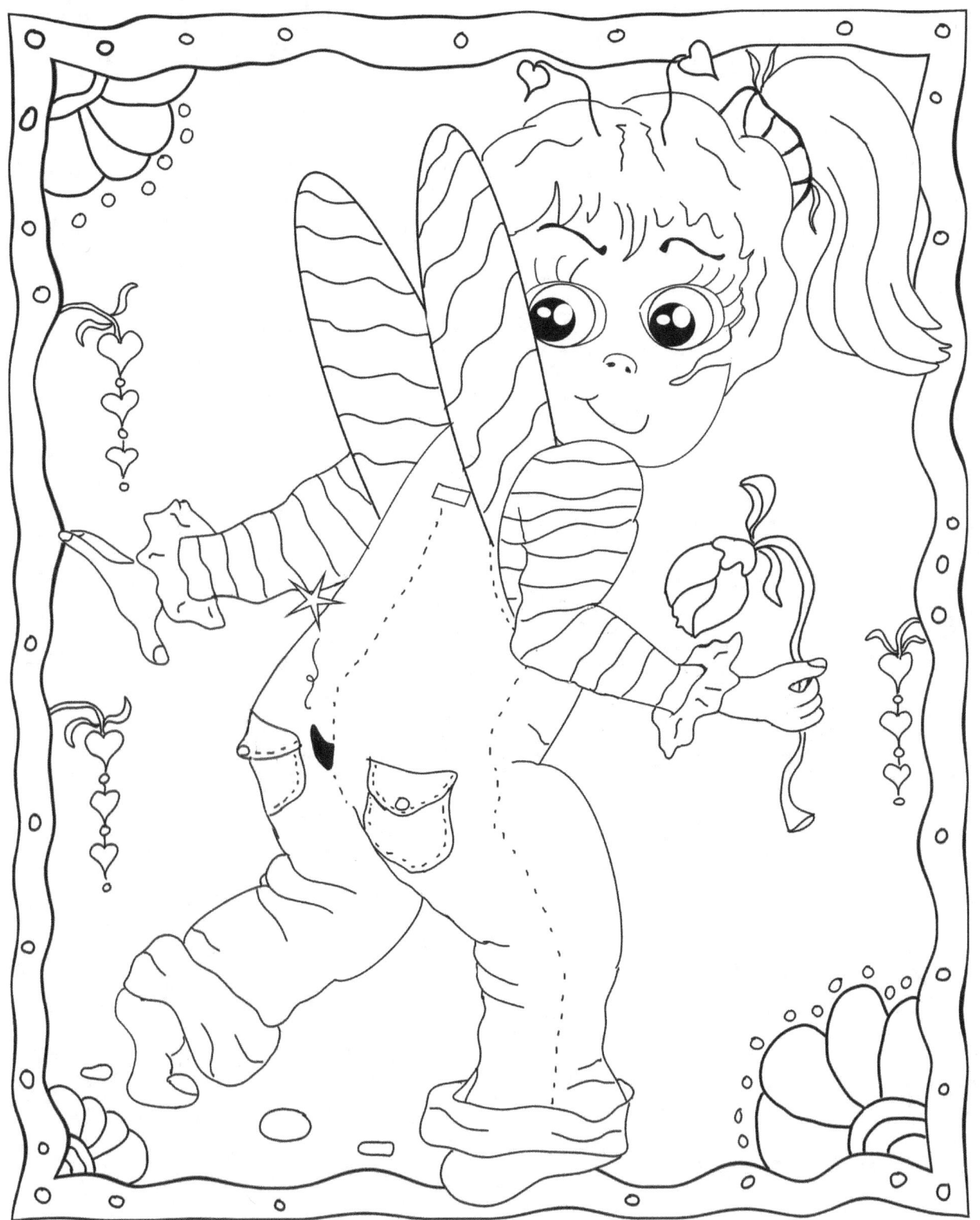

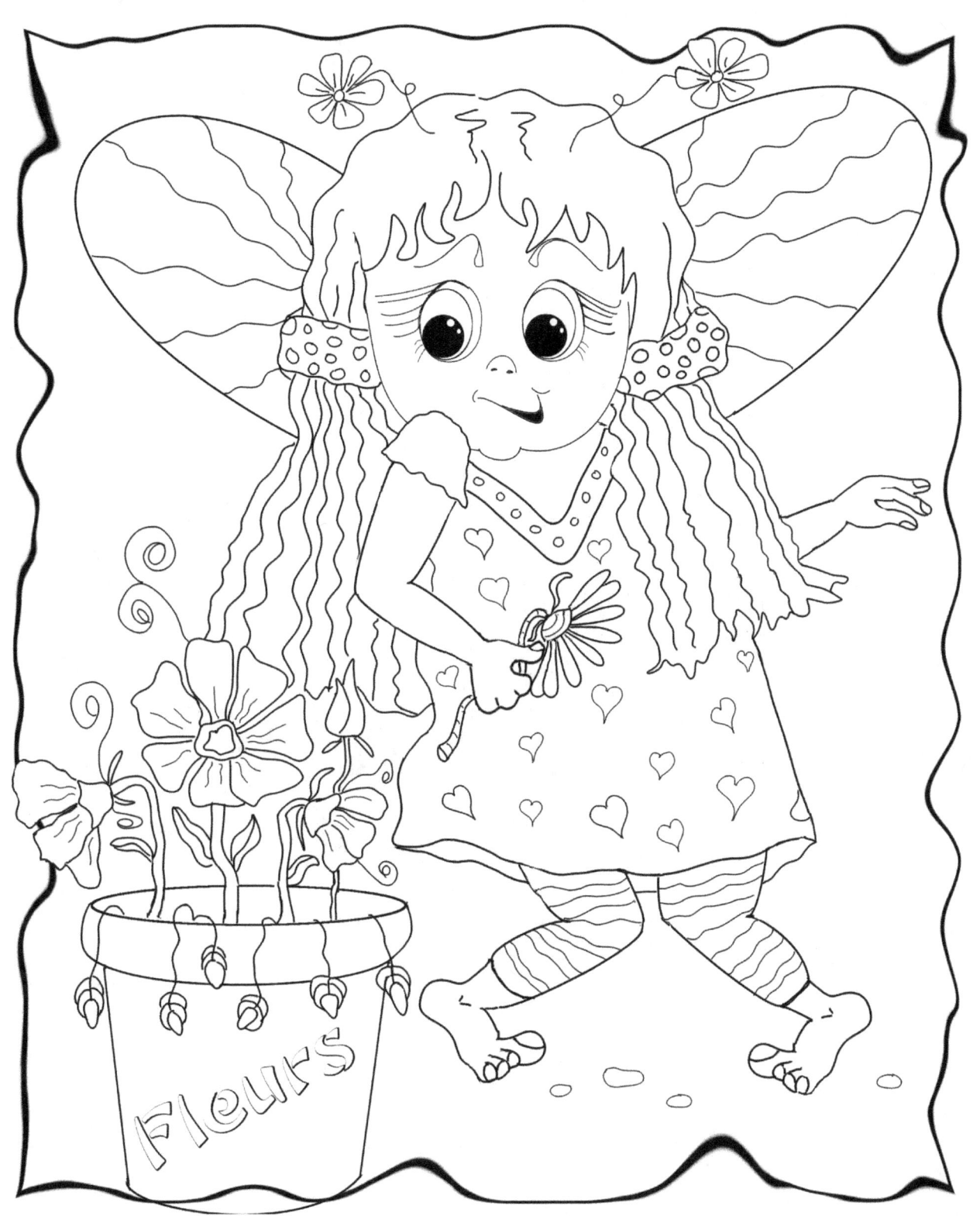

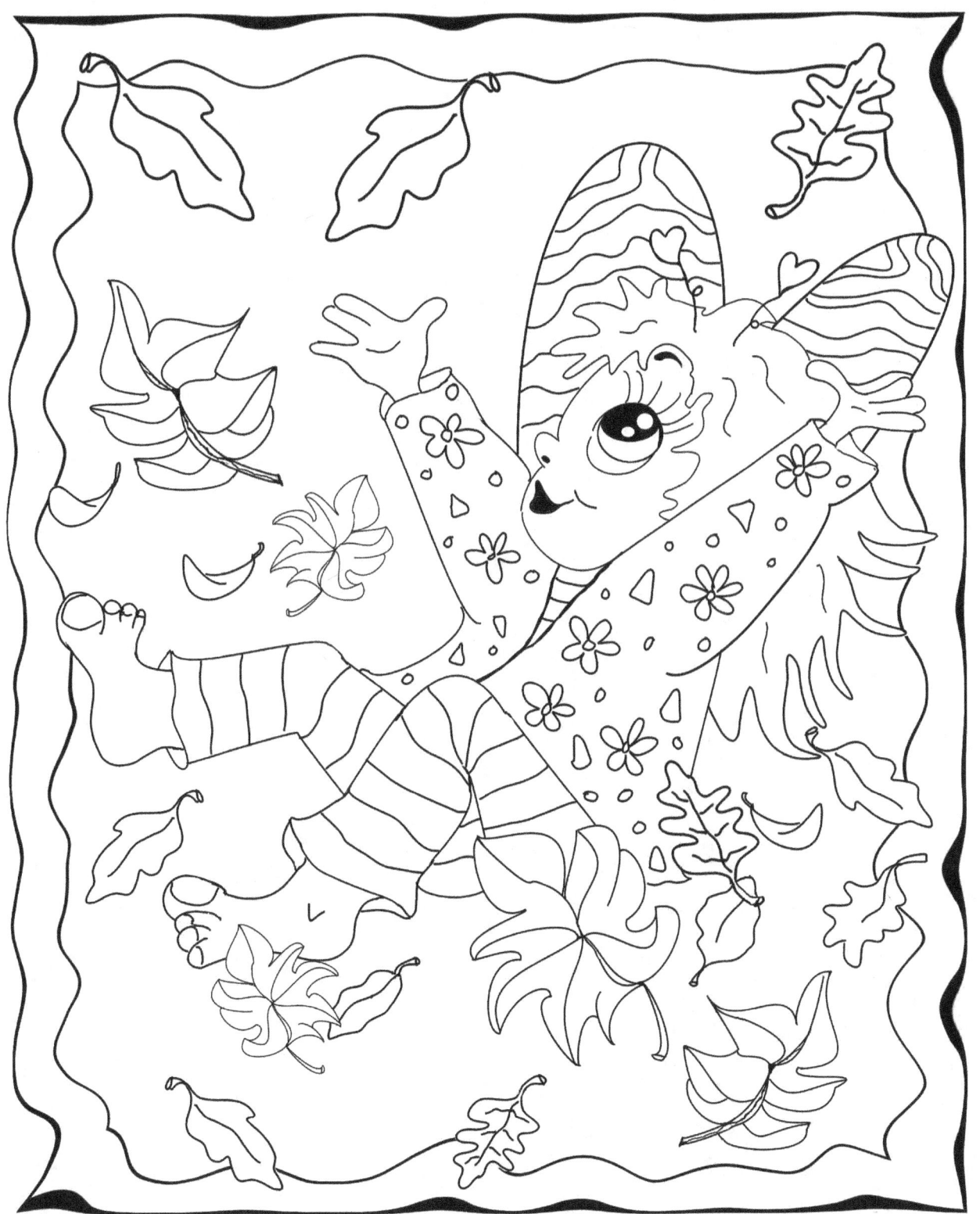

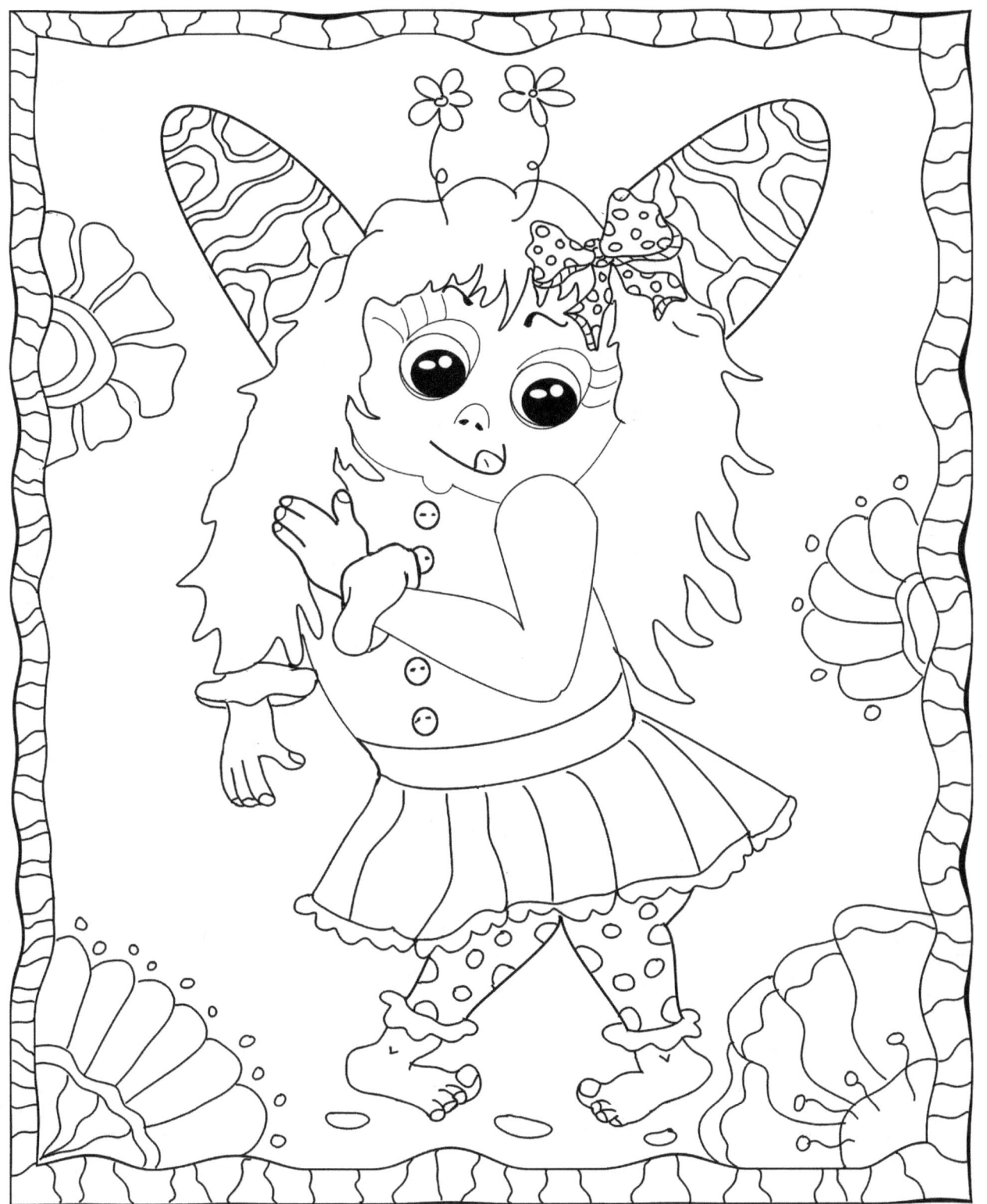

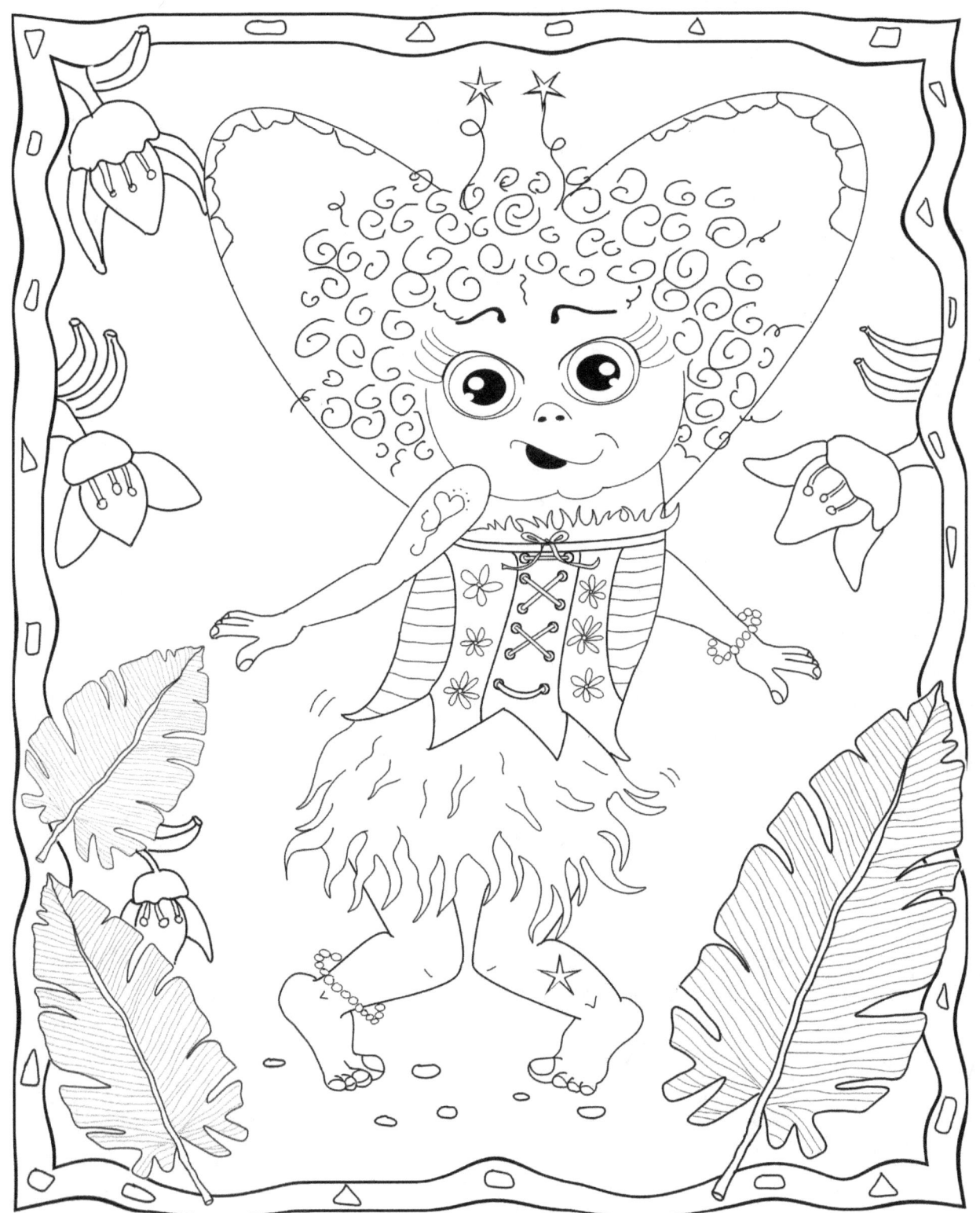

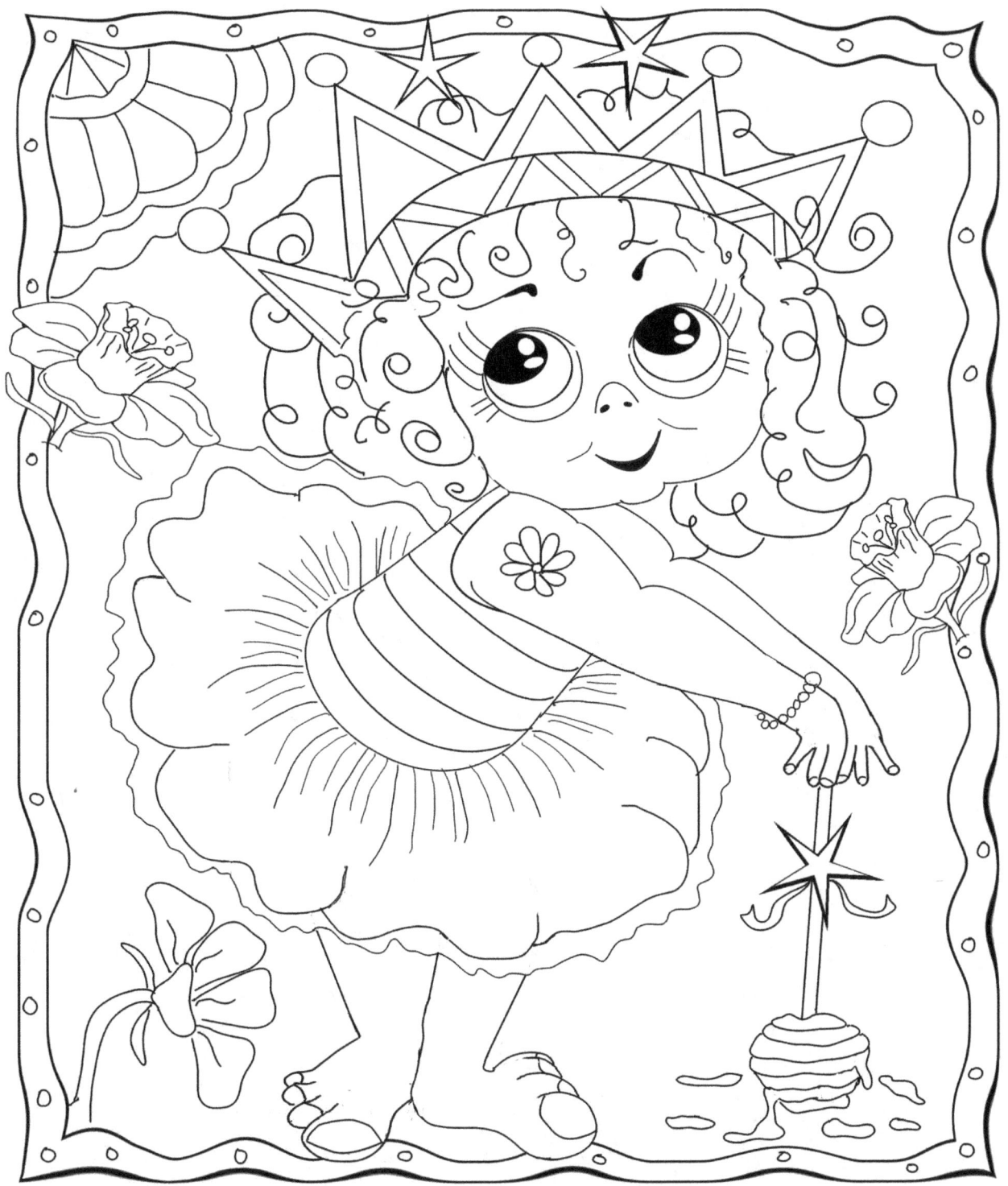

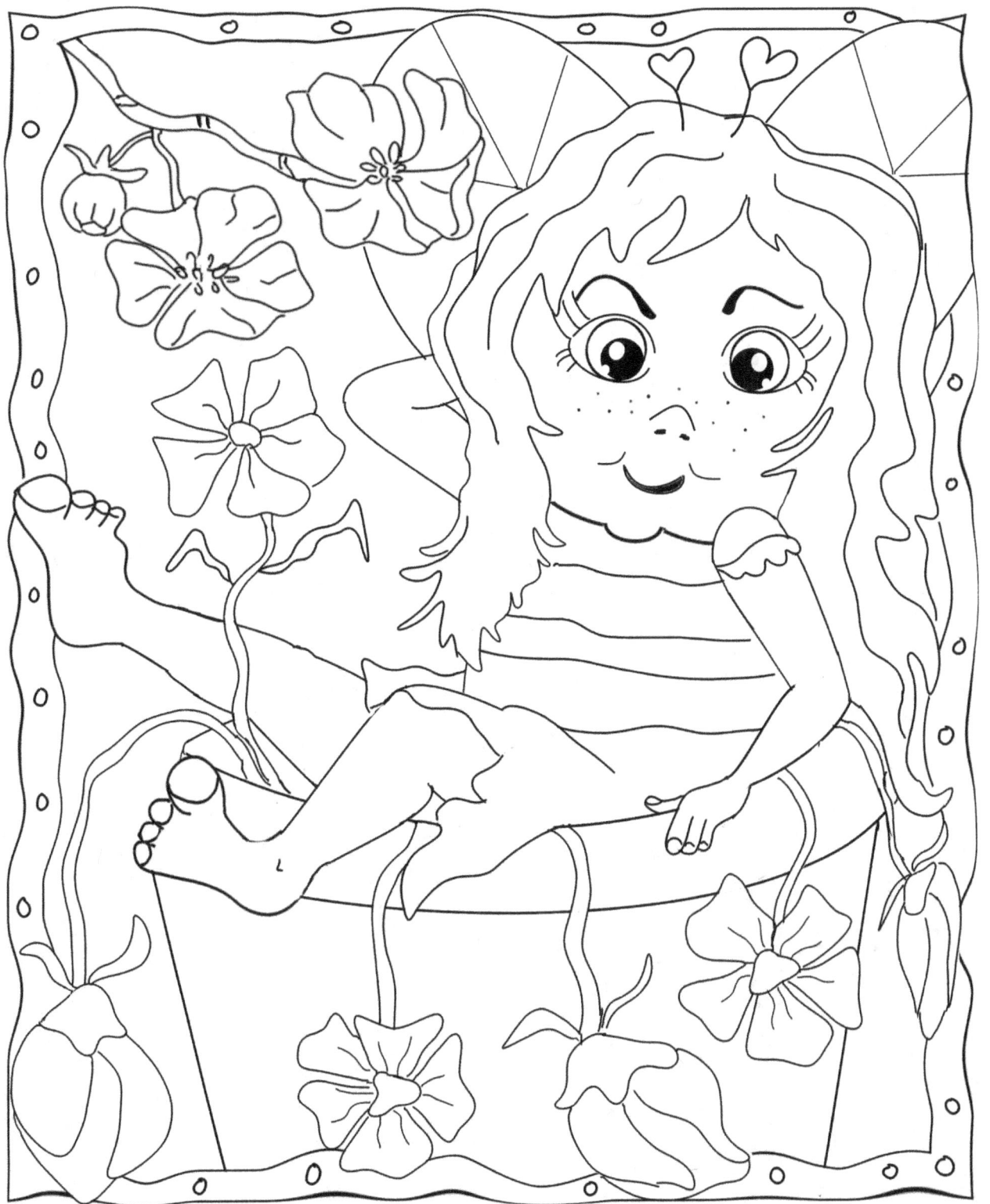

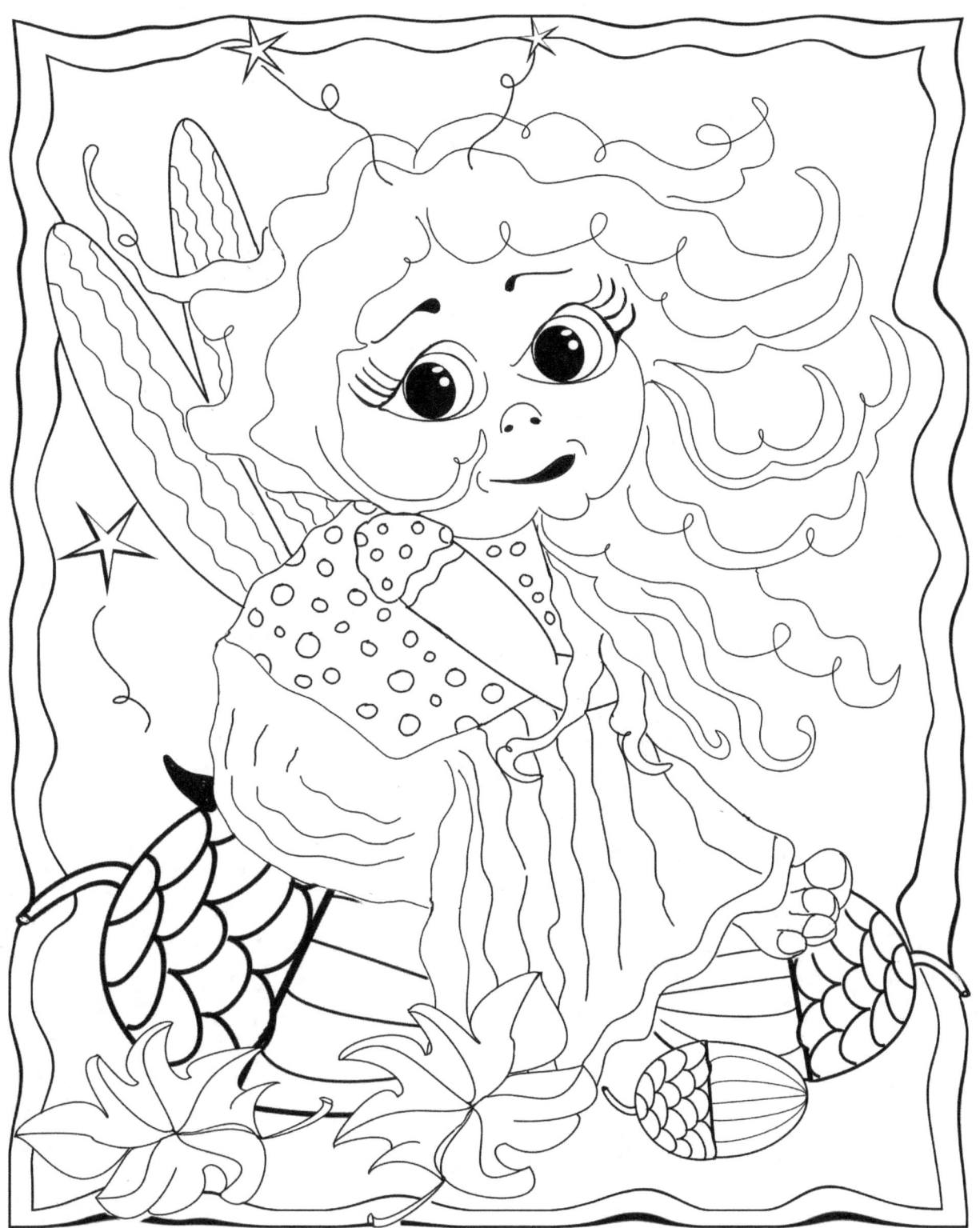

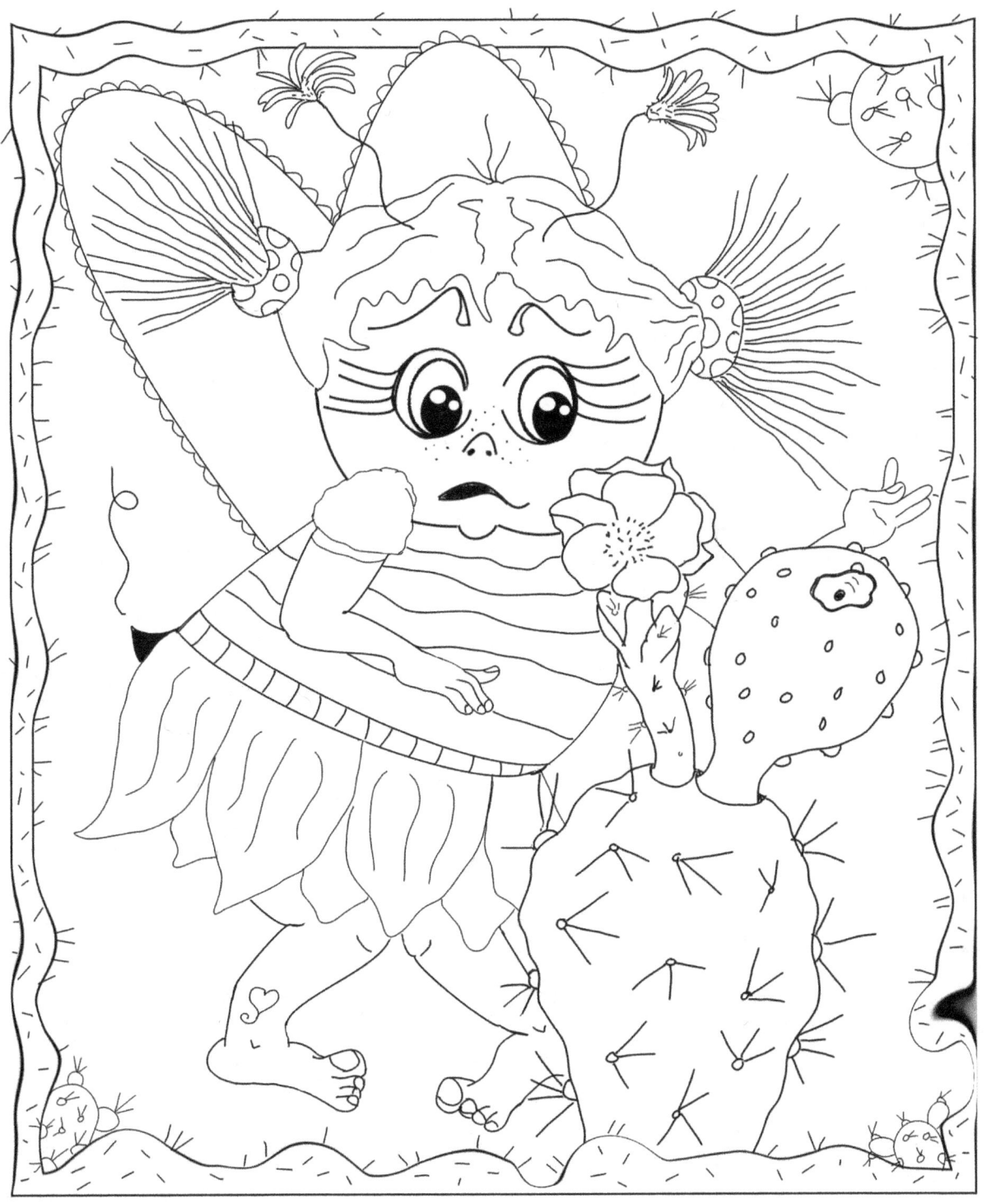

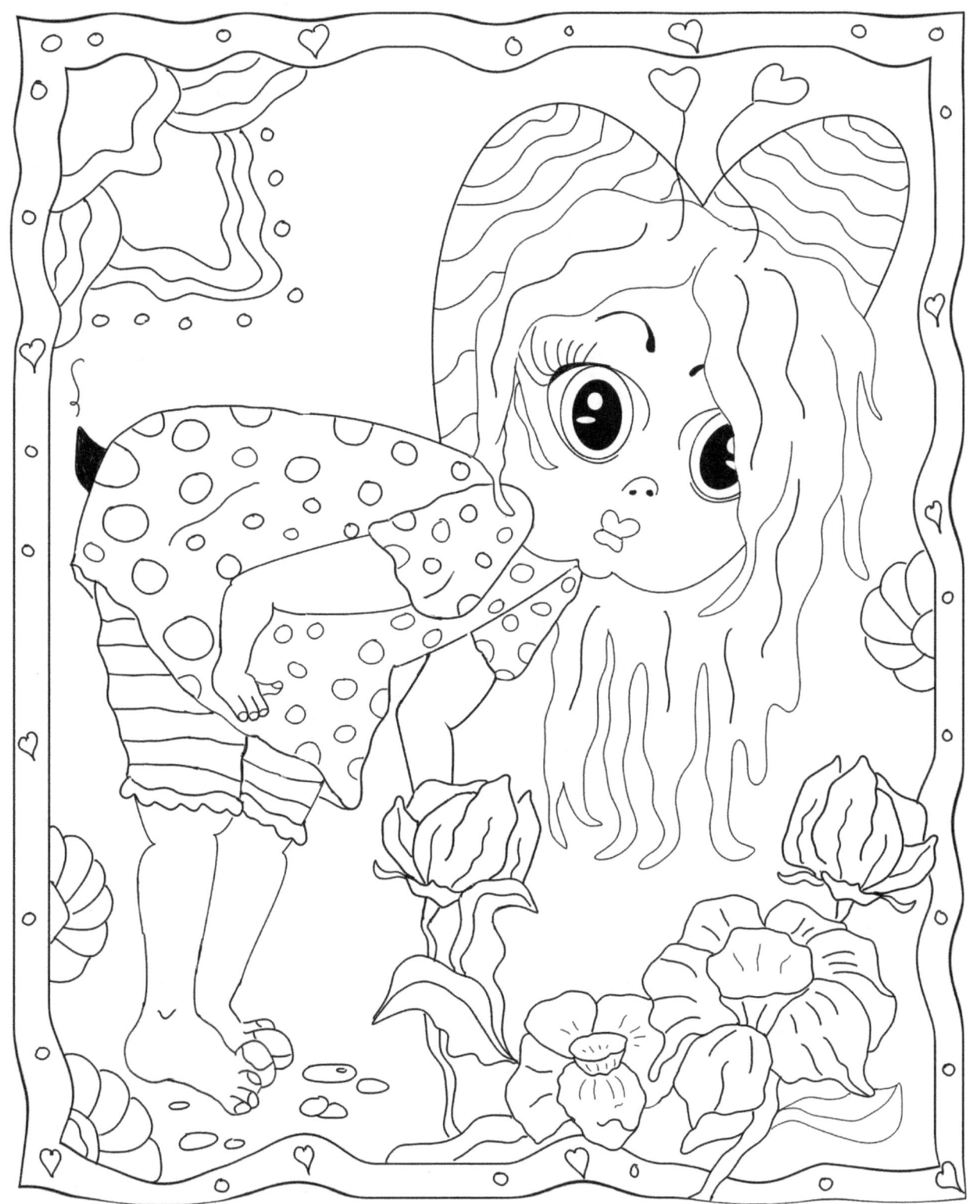

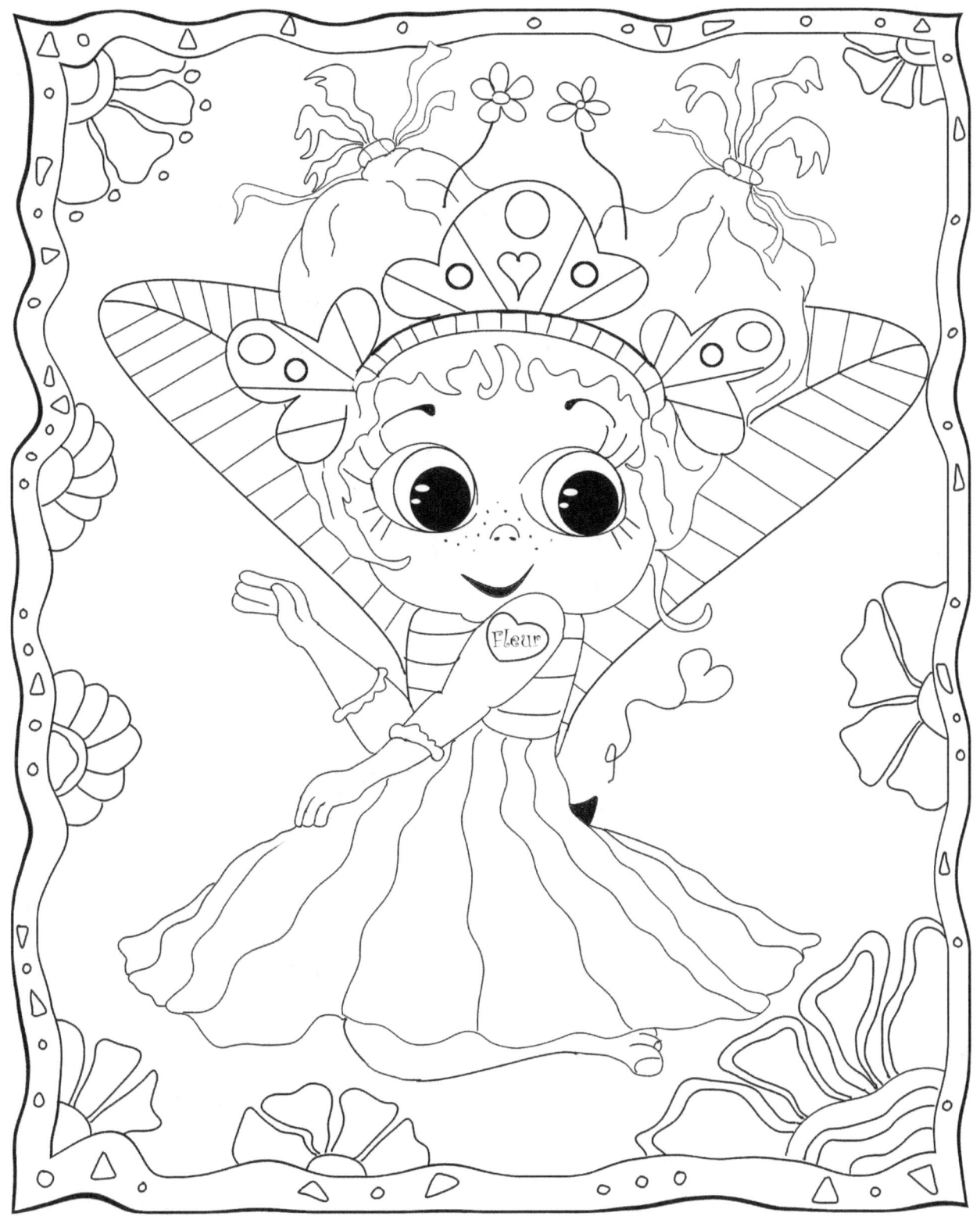

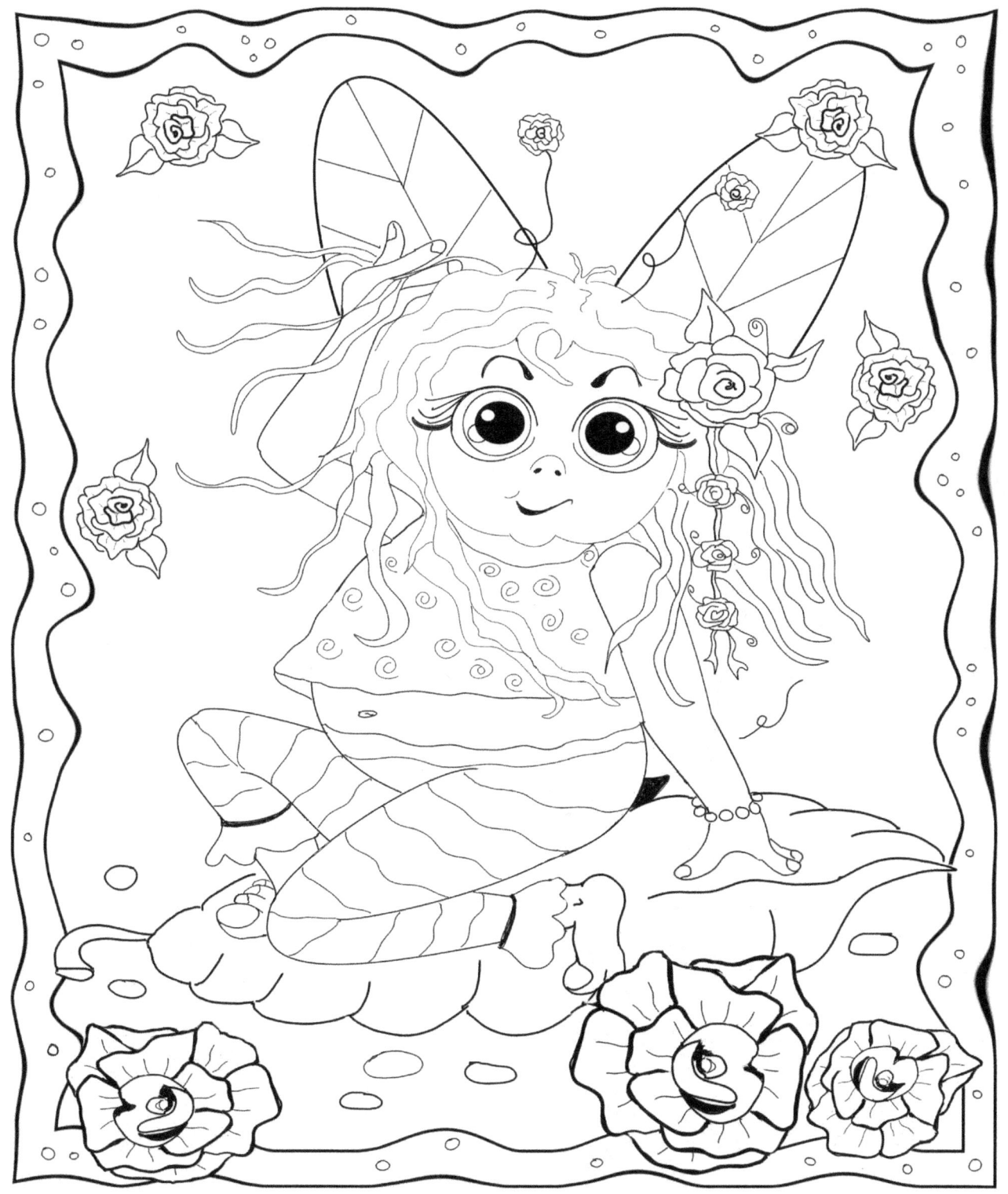

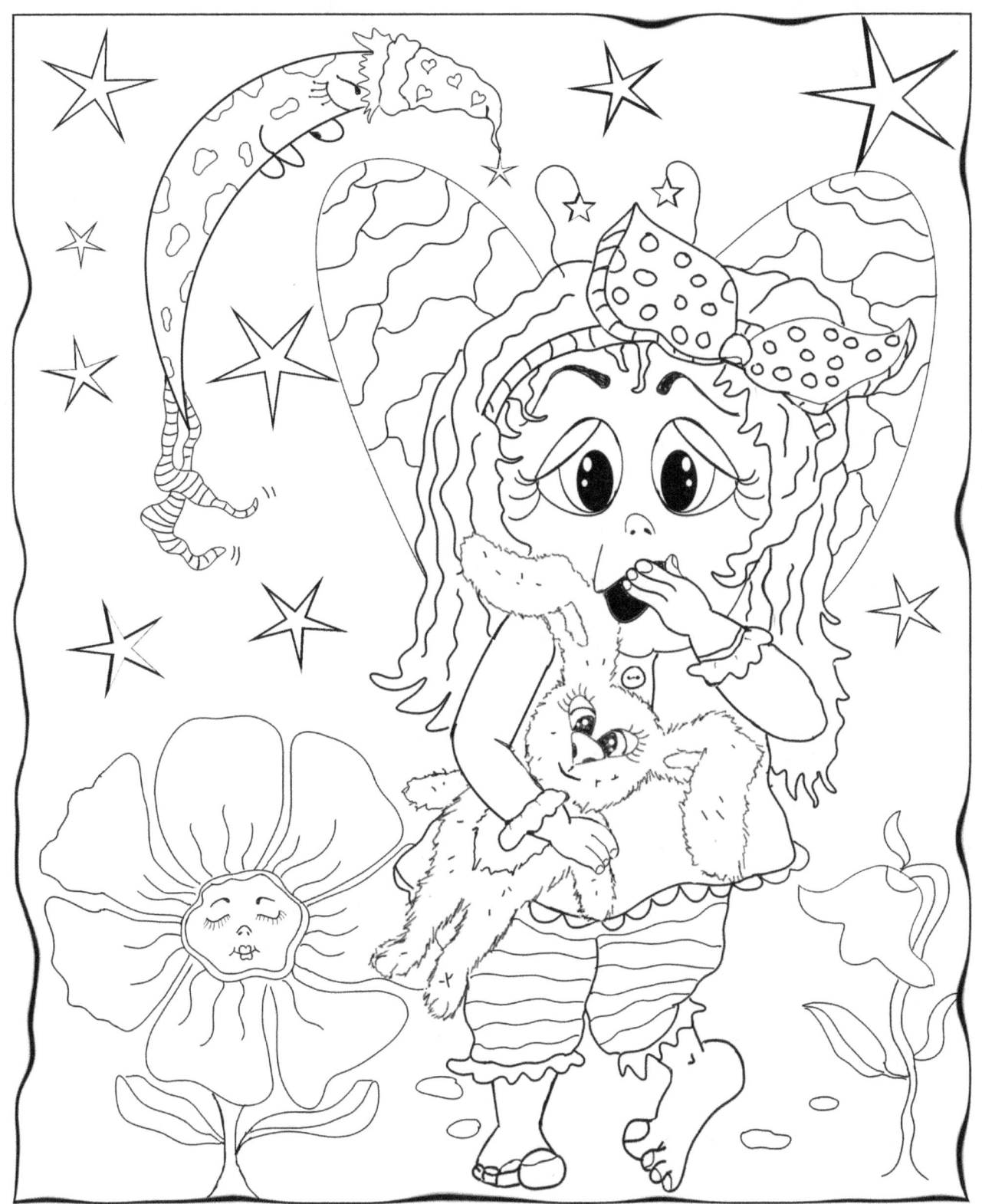

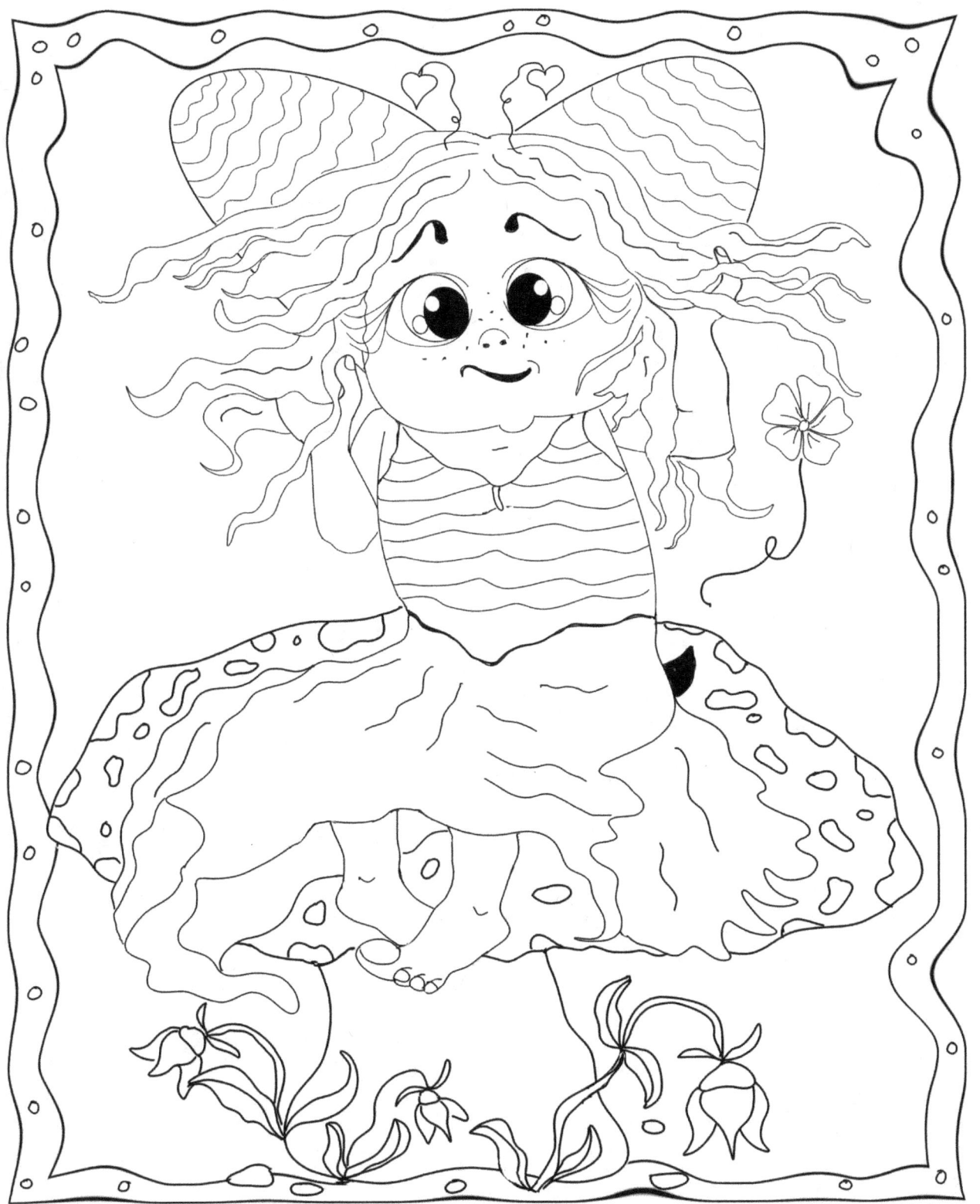

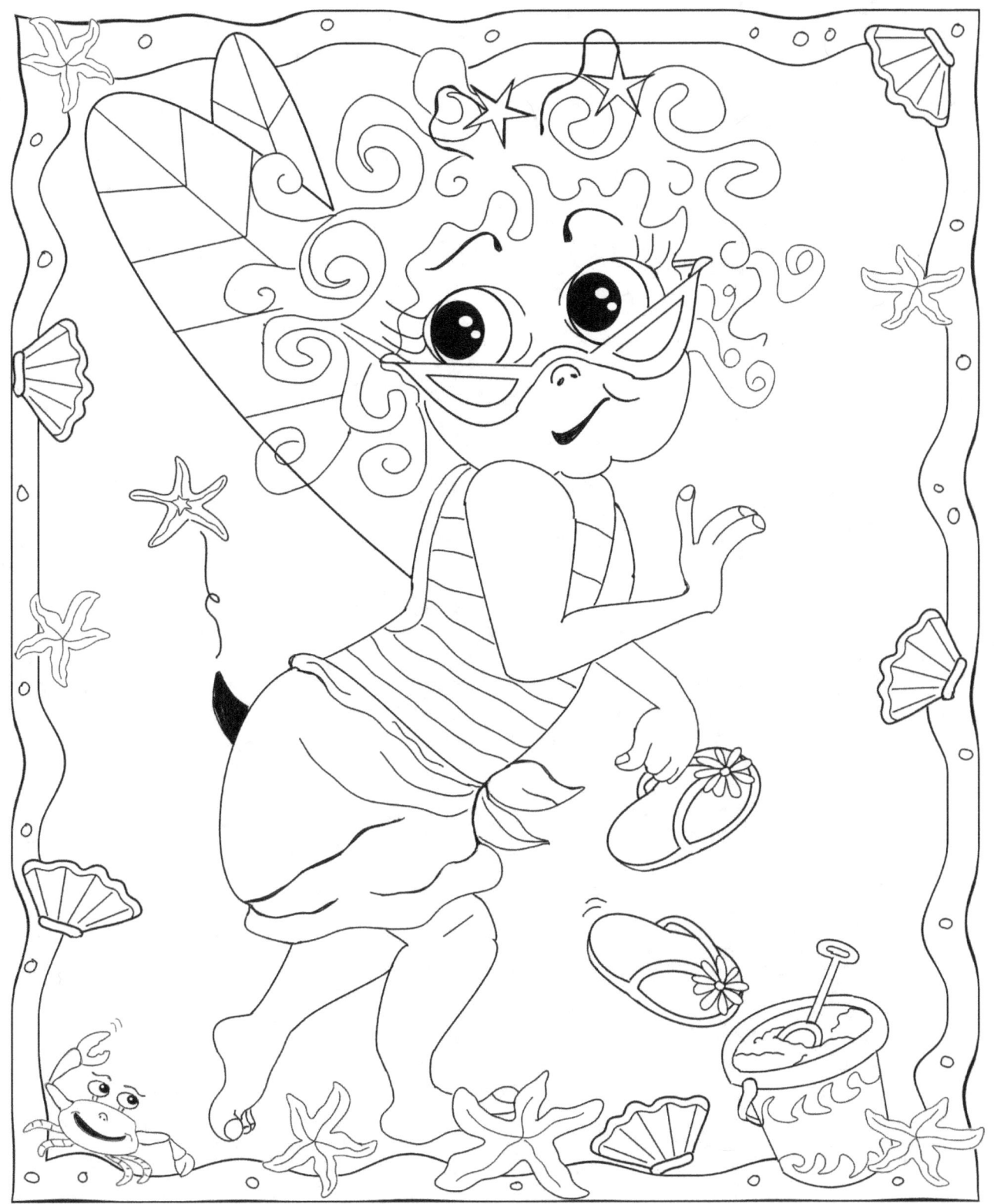

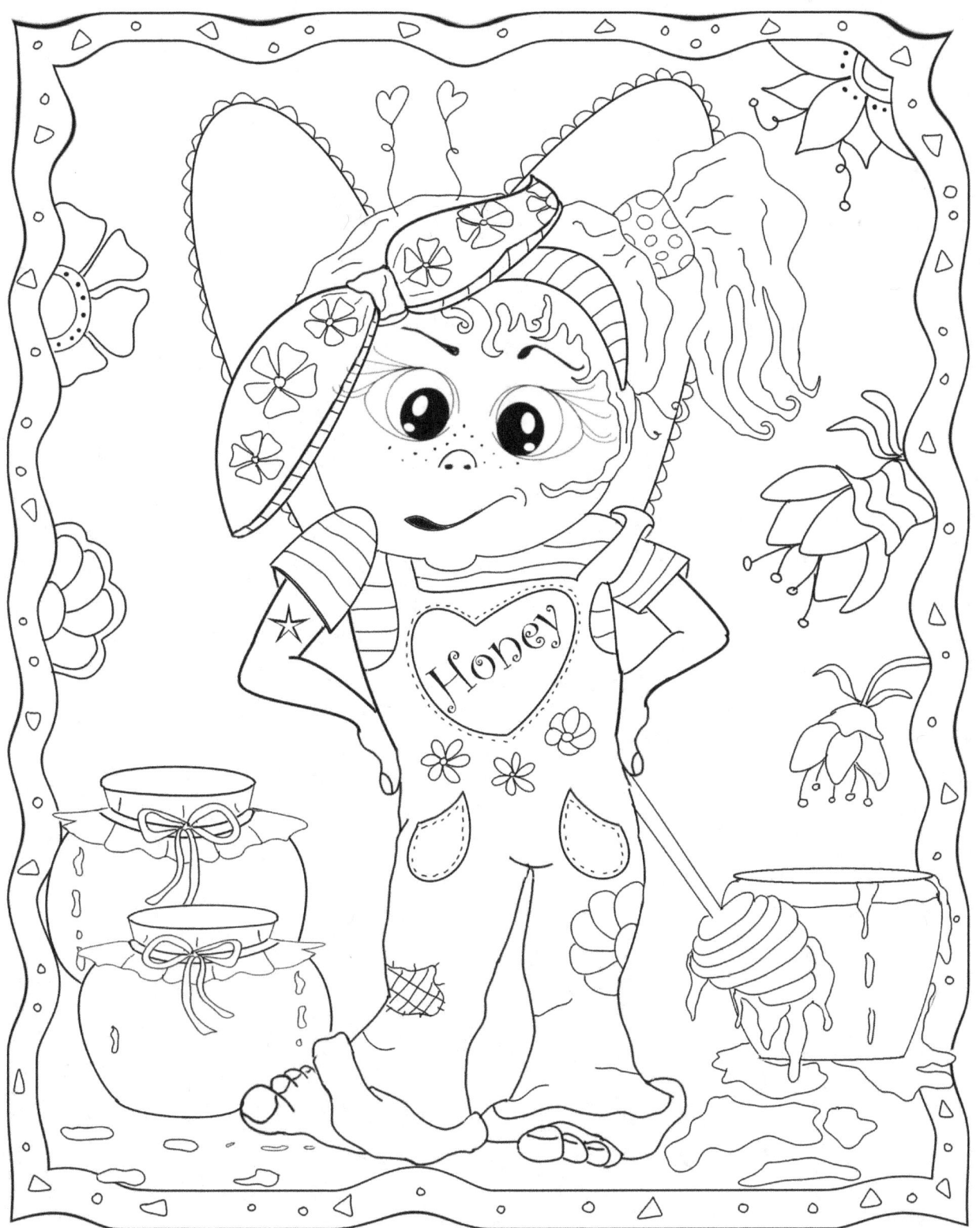

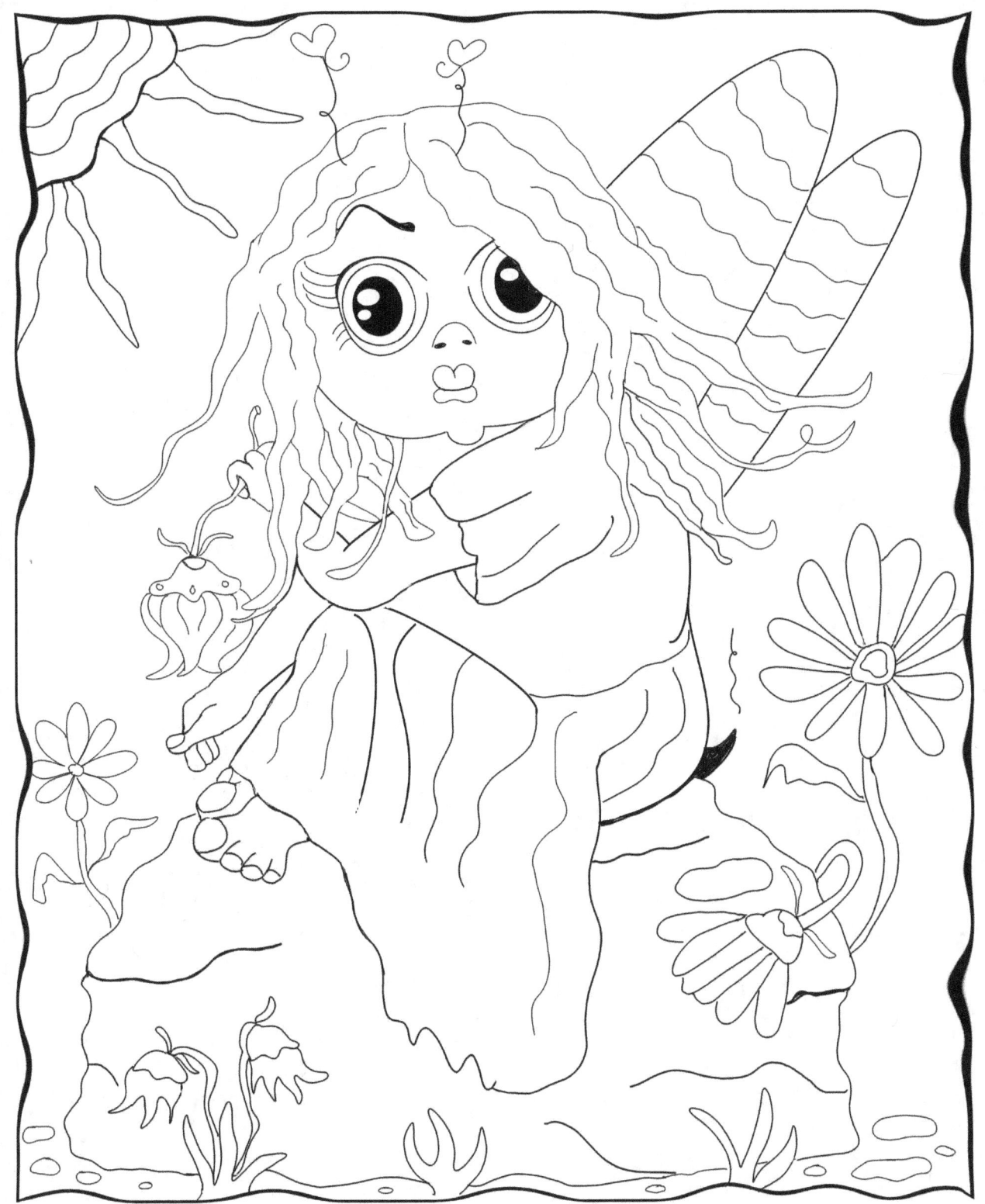

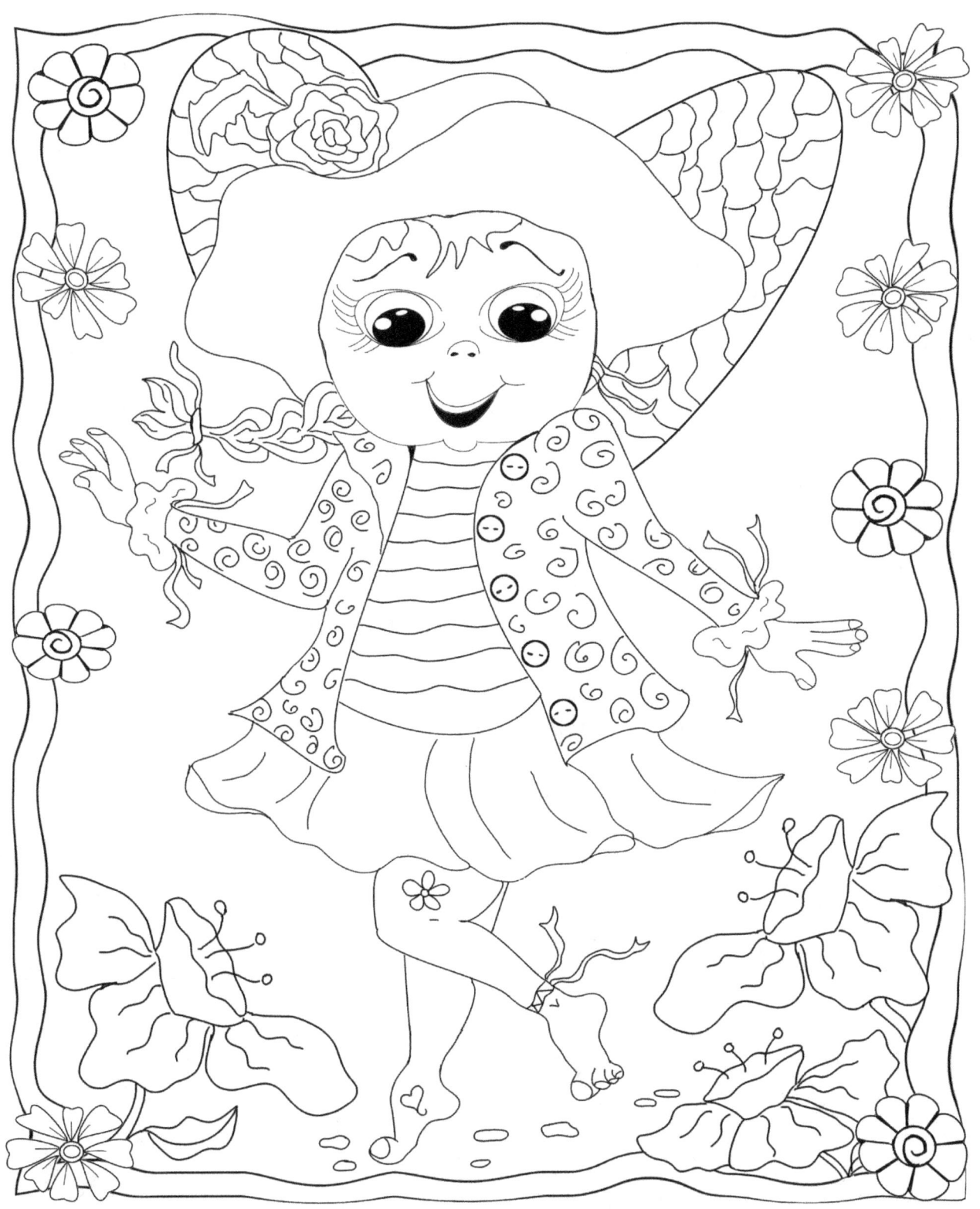

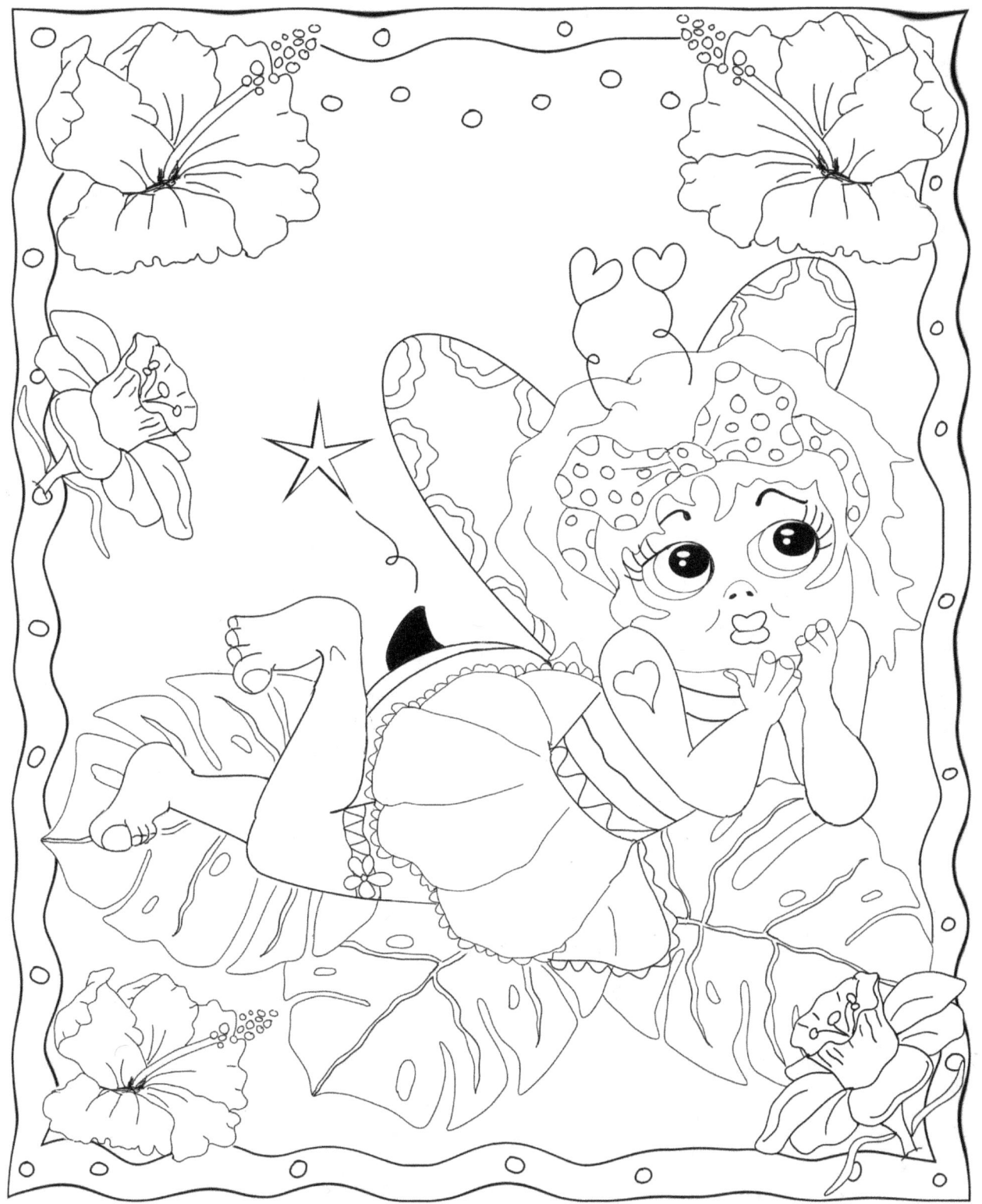

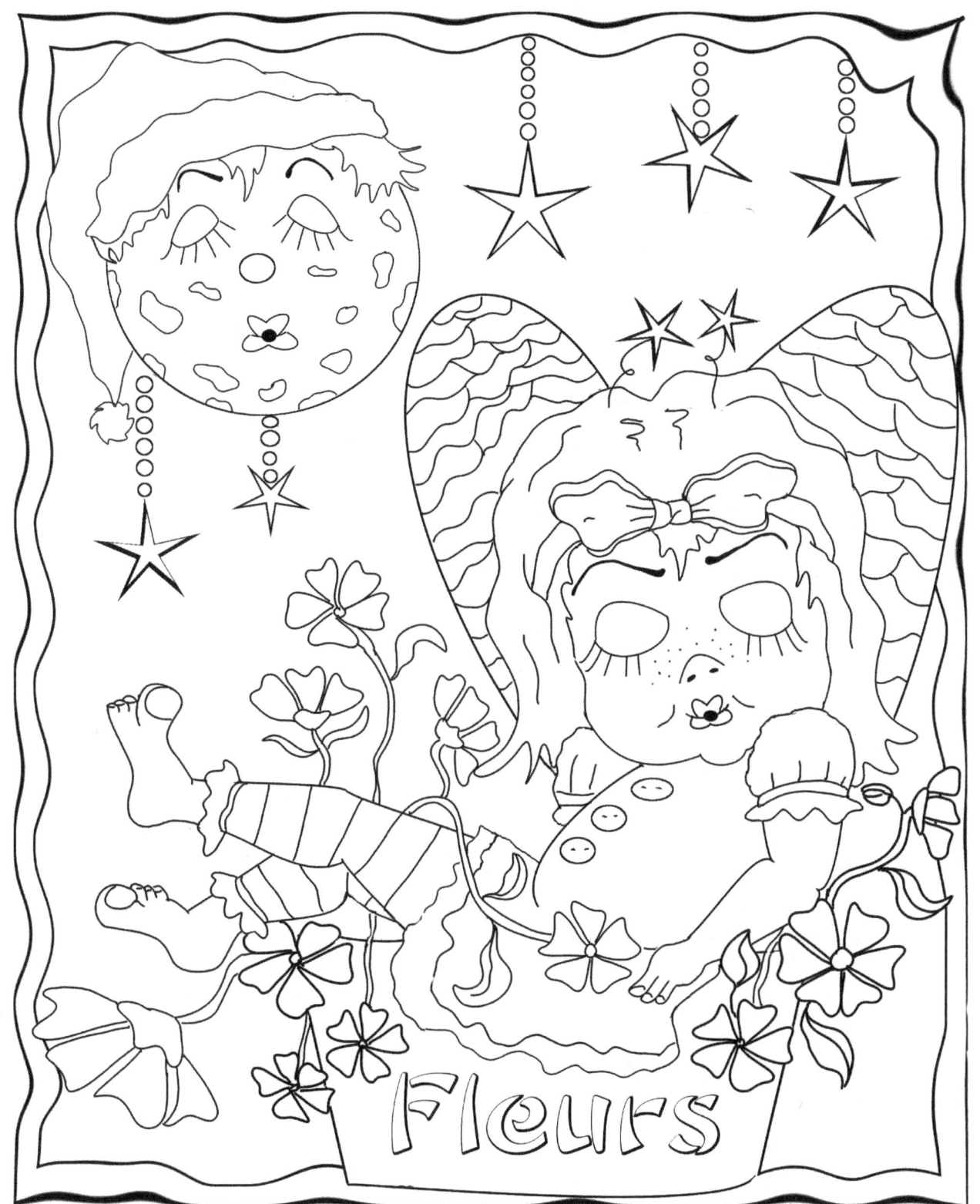

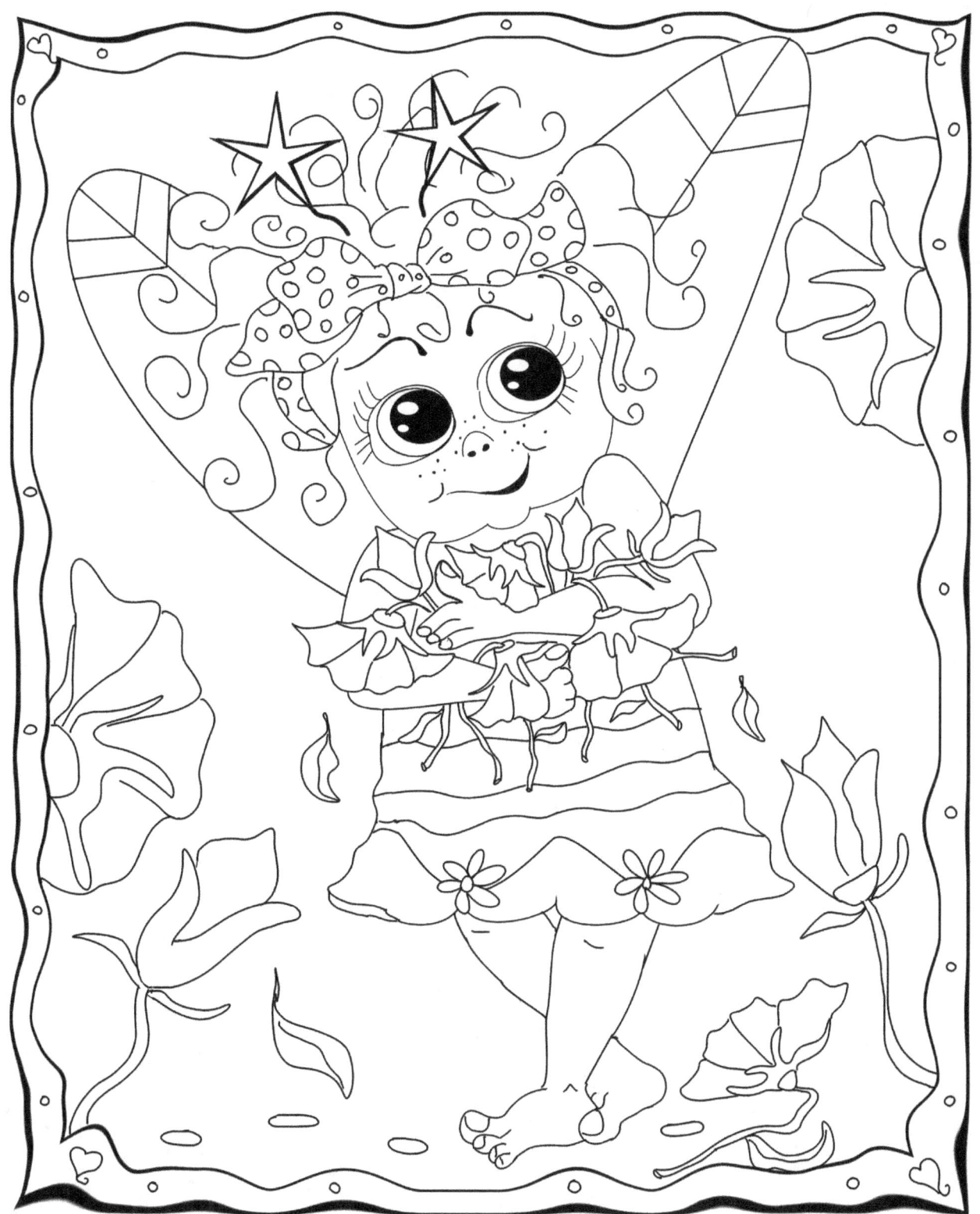

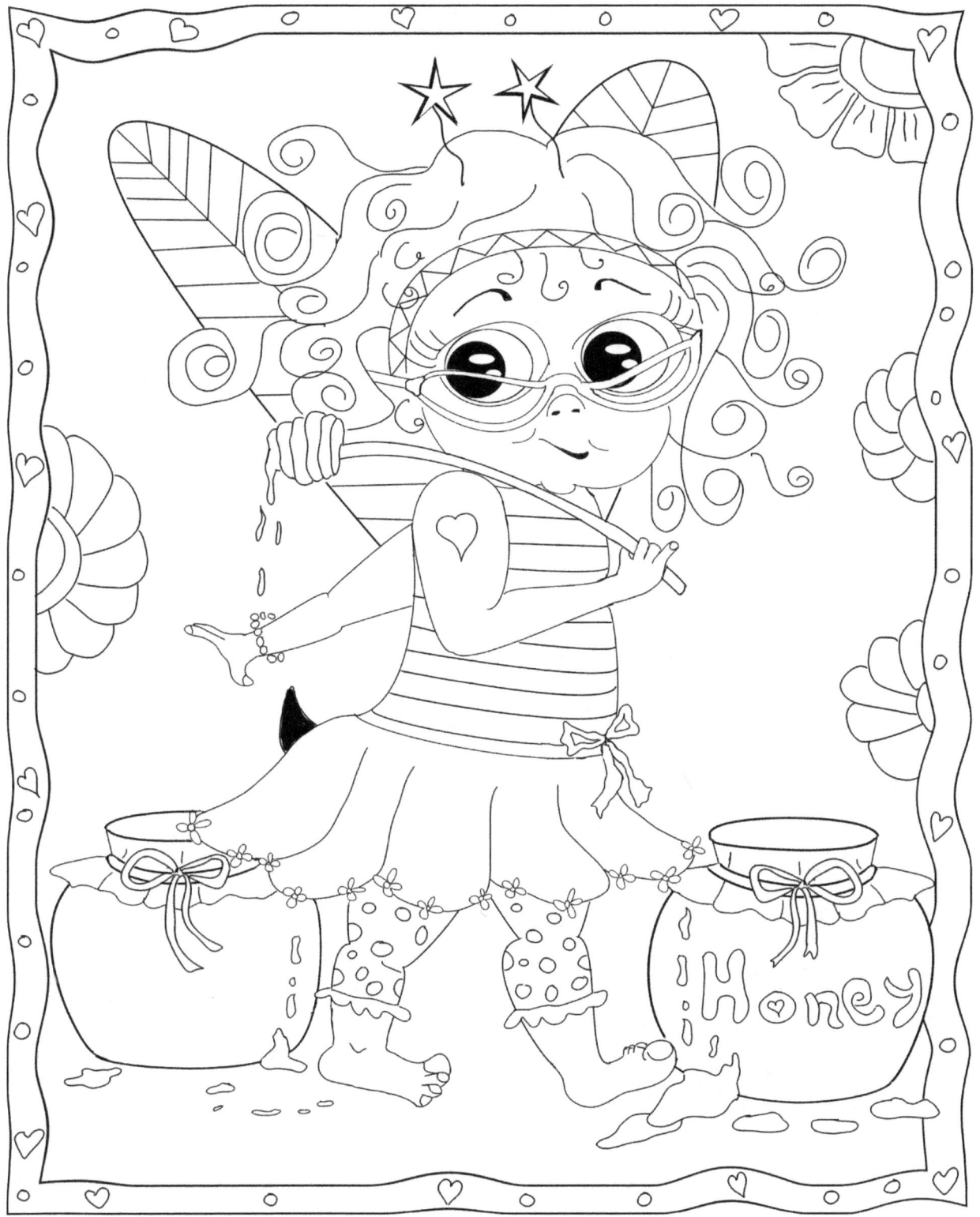

www.ingramcontent.com/pod-product-compliance
Lightning Source LLC
Chambersburg PA
CBHW082218220526
45470CB00010B/3218